AF399290
The Forgotten Gods

Emmy Sollien

THE FORGOTTEN GODS

-Reclaiming The Wisdom Of The Damned

TABLE OF CONTENTS

Thank you

I would like to extend my deepest gratitude to you, the reader, for buying this book and embarking on this journey through the forgotten realms of demonic wisdom and ancient knowledge. Your curiosity and openness to explore these complex and often misunderstood entities has made this work possible.

To the demons who have guided me with their wisdom and illuminated the path ahead, I thank you for your support and inspiration. This book is as much yours as it is mine.

To my family who always stand by me, my friends who support me and believe in what I do.

May the knowledge shared within these pages serve as a beacon on your spiritual journey, and may you find strength and wisdom in the forgotten gods.

Introduction

If you've found this text, you are likely drawn to the fascinating world of demons. You've come to the right place. This book traces the complex and often misunderstood history of these powerful beings, focusing on their transformation from gods of ancient pantheons to demons and angels, as shaped by the religious and political agendas throughout history.

Long before the Bible was even imagined, the people of the Ancient Near East worshiped a multitude of deities. These gods, revered for their roles in the natural and supernatural realms, were often seen as protectors, rulers, or symbols of power. But over time, as the beliefs of these people merged with evolving religious narratives, many of these gods would be redefined. As Christianity took root and spread, these ancient figures were repurposed to fit a new worldview—gods became demons, angels, and malevolent spirits to align with the moral framework that Christianity sought to establish.

This process of redefinition did not happen overnight. It was driven by centuries of conquest, cultural exchange, and theological debate. From the rise of the Hebrew Bible to the establishment of Christian doctrine, ancient gods were stripped of their divine status and recast as figures of evil. In this book, we will explore these shifts, focusing not just on the transformation of these beings, but on the larger forces at play that turned gods into demons.

As we journey through the origins of these beings, we will uncover the layers of myth, power, and ideology that shaped their legacy. The history of demons is not just about the fall from grace, but about how humanity's perception of the divine has evolved, from ancient civilizations to the complex theological debates of today.

This book draws on many sources, all of which are listed in the final chapter for your reference.

King Asmodius by Emmy Sollien©2023. Tarot of Hidden Knowledge

How to Use This Book

This book is designed to be both a guide and a companion. You do not have to read it from beginning to end in a linear fashion, although you are certainly welcome to. Feel free to jump between sections based on your current interest, need, or spiritual focus. Each chapter is meant to stand on its own while still contributing to the larger themes of transformation, history, and spiritual practice. Some chapters delve into historical or philosophical context, while others provide practical guidance for ritual, meditation, or shadow work. You are encouraged to take what resonates, reflect on it, and apply it in your own way. Demonolatry, like all spiritual paths, is deeply personal. Allow this book to serve as a mirror, a map, or even a gentle nudge toward your own truth.

Whether you are new to this path or well along your journey, may you find something here that illuminates your own connection to the forgotten gods.

While much of this book is rooted in historical research and comparative mythology, it also contains a significant amount of Unverified Personal Gnosis (UPG)—spiritual insights and experiences that come directly from my personal practice. These are not universally agreed upon truths but reflections of my unique relationship with the demons I work with, especially Azazel. They are included not to present a dogma, but to offer perspective, inspiration, and encourage others to cultivate their own gnosis through experience.

Ethics & Spiritual Responsibility Disclaimer

The practices and perspectives offered in this book are meant to empower, inspire, and inform. However, spiritual work, especially when engaging with spirits, demons, or archetypal energies, requires personal responsibility, discernment, and care.

This book does not promote coercion, manipulation, or the forced control of any spiritual being. Relationships with demons, like any sacred relationship, should be built on respect, consent, and mutual understanding. The techniques and philosophies presented here are offered as tools, not dogma, and should always be used in alignment with your ethical and spiritual integrity.

Additionally, spiritual practice is not a substitute for medical or psychological support. If you are experiencing mental health challenges, trauma, or emotional distress, please seek help from a licensed professional.

A Note on Language and Identity

Throughout this book, I use gendered pronouns for demons (such as he/him or she/her), often based on traditional sources or personal gnosis. However, it is important to remember that spiritual entities may transcend human concepts of gender. The language used here is a tool for communication and connection—not a limitation of their essence.

Feel free to engage with these beings in the way that feels most authentic to you. Some practitioners may experience certain demons as genderless, androgynous, or shifting. Your experience is valid.

As with all spiritual relationships, what matters most is sincerity, openness, and respect.

Author's Note on Religion

This book offers a critical exploration of the historical and cultural forces—particularly those rooted in Christianity—that contributed to the demonization of ancient deities, spirits, and practices. These critiques are aimed at institutional structures and dogmatic interpretations, not at individuals of faith or spirituality in general.

I fully respect the personal beliefs of others, including those who find deep meaning in Christianity or any other tradition. My intention is not to discredit religion itself, but to challenge narratives that have been used to suppress knowledge, marginalize spiritual practitioners, and distort the image of beings now labeled as "demons."

This work reflects my personal experiences, research, and spiritual path as a witch and demonolater. It is written for those seeking to reclaim forgotten wisdom, explore spiritual autonomy, and deepen their understanding of the complex relationship between humanity and the divine—however one defines it.

Dedicated To Lord Azazel

Commander of the Infernal Army

Lord Azazel by Emmy Sollien©2023

About the Author

Born and raised in Sweden, Emmy Sollien grew up in a nonreligious household, but from an early age felt an unshakable pull toward myth, magic, and the mysteries that lie just beyond the veil. Drawn especially to Norse mythology and the ancient stories of gods, giants, and spirits, Emmy's fascination with the unseen set the foundation for a lifelong spiritual journey.

That path eventually led them into the realms of the occult, where they embraced the identities of witch and demonolater—titles that reflect both devotion and defiance. Choosing to walk a road often shrouded in fear and misunderstanding, Emmy dedicated themselves to exploring the darker aspects of spirituality: demons, forgotten gods, shadow work, and the reclamation of ancient wisdom once deemed forbidden.

In The Forgotten Gods – Reclaiming the Wisdom of the Damned, Emmy weaves together historical research, mythological insight, and personal gnosis to reframe how we view demons—not as mere tempters or terrors, but as beings of profound depth, power, and transformation. With a voice both scholarly and soul-baring, they offer readers an invitation to challenge inherited fears and step into a relationship with the beings who have long waited in the shadows. At the heart of this work stands Emmy's deep and ongoing connection to Lord Azazel—a bond that has shaped their spiritual path and creative life in ways beyond words. As mentor, teacher, and sacred ally, Azazel has guided Emmy through personal growth, psychic awakening, and the development of spiritual tools such as tarot, visual alchemy, and magical art.

Through years of trust, challenge, and transformation, Azazel has not only inspired the writing of this book, but also stood as a companion through Emmy's darkest nights and most luminous revelations. This work is, in many ways, a tribute to him—a record of devotion, curiosity, and the power of walking the path less traveled.

With this book, Emmy seeks to share the wisdom of the damned, and offer it back to the world—not in fear, but in fire.

"To be understood by a human so deeply is an honor that I cannot express through words alone."

-Lord Azazel

1. THE RISE OF THE FALLEN - THE BIRTH OF DEMONS

Long before the concept of a singular, all-powerful god dominated religious thought, the people of the ancient world understood the divine as a complex network of beings, each with specific powers over different aspects of life and nature. These gods were not seen as inherently good or evil; they simply were. They ruled over mountains, rivers, the sun, the harvest, and even death. Their personalities and actions, often unpredictable, reflected the chaos and wonder of the natural world.

In many cultures, however, these powerful deities would not remain in their positions forever. As societies evolved and new religious systems took hold, the gods of old were slowly redefined—often to fit new political or theological agendas. In time, societies transformed the revered gods into malevolent forces or fallen angels, their former divinity corrupted into symbols of evil.

Take, for example, the ancient gods of the Mesopotamians and the Canaanites. Figures like Baal, a storm god, and Yam, the god of the sea, held central roles in their respective pantheons, commanding respect and devotion. However, the biblical tradition reimagined Baal and similar deities as enemies of the one true God, viewing their powers not as divine authority but as a threat to righteousness. The process of demonization, which began in the ancient world, continued into the

Hebrew scriptures and beyond, transforming revered gods into demons whose stories would shape the religious imagination for centuries to come.

The shifting of gods into demonic figures is not limited to the Near East. In Greece, Rome, and even the Norse traditions, similar transformations happened throughout the ancient world. The prevailing religious and cultural climate often caused gods and spirits to shift between revered and feared figures, blurring the lines between divine and demonic.

This book will explore how and when these shifts happened, focusing on the story of the Watchers but also other gods who would eventually be recast as demons. Their stories reveal the earliest origins of our modern understanding of demons.

The Divine Council- The Gods who Once Ruled

Before the demonization, most gods were part of a larger, organized system—a Divine Council—in which various deities governed the cosmos collectively, each responsible for a specific domain. This concept, found in many ancient cultures, portrays gods as part of a heavenly assembly, working together to oversee the world.

In the ancient Near East, daily life intricately intertwined with the pantheons of gods, which governed both natural forces and the political and social order. These gods were not abstract or distant figures—they were deeply involved in the workings of the cosmos, the stability of kingdoms, and the destinies of nations.

At the heart of the Ugaritic pantheon stood El, the wise and fatherly deity who ruled over the divine council. El, a figure of eminent authority, led a council of lesser gods who served him in maintaining cosmic order. This divine assembly mirrors the structure seen in the Hebrew Bible's Divine Council, where gods deliberated on matters of human affairs, but El was the ultimate authority, overseeing the world with wisdom and care.

Across the larger godly world, a god's function was determined by the powers they personified. Yam, the sea, was synonymous with chaos, constantly in conflict with the storm gods like Baal and Marduk of Babylon, whose power to bring order from the chaos of the sea symbolized the ongoing battle between stability and disorder. Mot, the god of death, was an essential figure in the cycle of life and death. His battles with life-affirming gods reflected not only the literal cycles of nature but also the profound existential struggles humans faced in the face of mortality.

The pantheon held more significance than just theological or mythical ideas; Deities like Ashur in Assyria were not just gods of nature—they were intimately tied to military conquest and the expansion of empires. Kings saw themselves as divinely chosen, often aligned with their city's patron deity to legitimize their reign and victories.

Across different cultures in the Ancient Near East, the concept of a divine council was widespread. In the Ugaritic texts, the council of El comprised 70 divine beings who assisted him in overseeing the cosmos, each deity playing a crucial role. Similarly, in Mesopotamian texts like the Enuma Elish, gods gathered in assemblies to deliberate over matters of divine and earthly importance. The chief deity, such as El or Marduk, had the final say in these deliberations, their decisions shaping the course of history.

In Egypt, the divine assembly was also integral to the functioning of the cosmos. Figures like Ra and Osiris presided over gatherings of gods who judged human actions and settled disputes among themselves. This divine council helped maintain ma'at, the concept of cosmic order, which was crucial to Egyptian belief systems.

In the ancient world, the divine realm wasn't distant or abstract—it was alive with politics, power, and presence. The pantheons of the Ancient Near East mirrored the human world, with gods who debated, clashed, and ruled in councils.

These divine assemblies weren't just spiritual metaphors; they reflected how people understood law, justice, kingship, and the fragile balance between order and chaos.

Early Israelite belief echoed this structure. Yahweh was not always envisioned as the sole deity, but as the high god among a host of divine beings. Passages like Psalm 82 preserve a glimpse of this older vision:

"God stands in the divine assembly; He gives judgment among the gods."

In these lines, Yahweh judges—not demons—but fellow gods, chastising them not for being evil, but for failing in their sacred duty to uphold justice. Over time, this vision began to change. In the wake of exile, upheaval, and reform, Israel's theology turned toward a stricter monotheism. The old gods were not entirely discarded—they were transformed. Some were renamed angels, divine messengers stripped of their former sovereignty. Others, like Azazel, became demons: cast down, feared, and vilified. But their roots run deep. And understanding where they came from lets us reclaim what was lost—not to return to the past, but to see the full spectrum of what divinity once meant.

As monotheism took hold—especially with the rise of Christianity—the old celestial hierarchies were rewritten. Gods who once ruled the skies, the waters, the forests, and the stars were reimagined, recast, or erased. No longer divine rulers in their own right, they became rebellious spirits, fallen angels, or outright demons.

This wasn't just a theological shift—it was a total restructuring of how the sacred was understood. One god now ruled all. And the rest? They were silenced, subordinated, or vilified.

Texts like 1 Enoch give us a clear window into this transformation. The Watchers, once part of the divine order, fall not because they are evil by nature, but because they dared to cross divine boundaries. They descended, loved, taught, and shared. For that, they were cast down. What was once divine intimacy became taboo. What was once sacred knowledge became forbidden.

This story—of gods becoming demons, of sacred beings turned into villains—didn't happen overnight. It was a long and layered process, driven by politics, theology, and the desire to control religious narratives.

The ancient Divine Council, once a chorus of distinct powers and presences, was dismantled to make room for a singular, absolute ruler.

But these fallen figures didn't disappear. They linger in the margins of scripture, in whispers of older myths, in the names that still echo in ritual and spellwork today. For us—pagans, witches, and occult practitioners—understanding this shift isn't just historical. It's a way to reclaim what was lost. To see the divine not as a single throne in the sky, but as a web of beings who once held power, wisdom, and presence. Some were called angels. Some were called demons. But before all that, they were gods.

In the earliest layers of scripture, we find hints of a more complex divine world—one where beings like the bene Elohim, the "sons of God" mentioned in Genesis 6:2, moved freely between realms. These figures were once seen as divine, perhaps even gods in their own right. But as Israelite religion grew more monotheistic, these beings were rebranded: not gods, but angels. Not equals, but servants.

The gods of neighboring cultures suffered an even harsher fate. Take Baal, for example—a storm god, worshipped widely across Canaan. In older texts, he was powerful, sacred. But in the eyes of the emerging Israelite religion, he became a threat. Over time, Baal was demonized— transformed into a symbol of idolatry, even linked with Satanic forces. This wasn't just theology—it was strategy. By casting rival gods as evil, Israelite leaders could delegitimize competing religions and centralize power around Yahweh.

But this story is more tangled than a simple "us versus them." Israel's faith didn't grow in isolation. It was shaped by its neighbors—Babylon, Persia, and others. From Babylon, they absorbed myths and cosmology. From Persia, especially during the Exile, came a sharper sense of dualism: a cosmic divide between good and evil. Zoroastrian influence can be felt in the clear-cut lines later drawn between angels and demons.

Scholars of ancient religion recognize that Yahweh, the god of Israel, did not appear fully formed as a strict monotheistic figure. Early Israelite religion likely included polytheistic elements — with Yahweh originally seen as one god among others, possibly a storm or warrior deity associated with specific regions (like Edom or Seir). Over time, Yahweh absorbed attributes of other gods, most notably El, the chief god of the Canaanite and Ugaritic pantheons, who was seen as the high father, the wise elder. This merging helped transition local worshippers toward a singular, unified deity.

There's also archaeological and textual evidence suggesting that Asherah, a mother goddess, was once venerated alongside Yahweh — inscriptions like *"Yahweh and his Asherah"* have been found on ancient altars. But as monotheism strengthened, these feminine or consort aspects were erased or demonized. This shift reflects the process of religious centralization and purification, where competing divine figures were absorbed, redefined, or discarded.

By the Second Temple period, the new order was in place. Angels like Michael and Gabriel held divine roles, but always in service to one god. Others were cast down, their stories echoing those of once-venerated deities. Texts like 1 Enoch and the Book of Jubilees sealed this transformation: the old gods became demons, their myths reimagined as tales of rebellion and punishment.

And this pattern wasn't unique to Israel. Zoroastrianism labeled rival gods as daevas—evil spirits. Christianity followed suit, turning the Greco-Roman gods into demons in the effort to stamp out paganism. Again and again, the divine was divided: light and dark, holy and wicked, worthy and cursed. But the bones of the old gods still show through. For those of us who walk the crooked path—witches, mystics, and seekers—these stories are invitations. To look past the labels. To hear the voices beneath the vilification. And to ask: Who were these beings before they were demonized? And what can they still teach us today?

Scholars like Mark S. Smith (The Early History of God) and Michael Heiser (The Unseen Realm) suggest that these shifts were not simple acts of rejection, but part of a larger pattern of theological transformation. Instead of erasing the old gods, ancient cultures often redefined them—lowering their rank, changing their names, folding them into new hierarchies as angels, demons, or divine servants.

This quiet reshaping wasn't just theological—it was deeply cultural. As civilizations in the Ancient Near East collided, overlapped, and evolved, so too did their visions of the sacred. The stories, symbols, and spirits that shaped the early polytheistic world didn't vanish. They were rewritten. Absorbed. Hidden in plain sight.

And from those transformations, the foundations of Judaism, Christianity, and Islam would later rise—built on layers of older belief, forgotten names, and once-revered gods now wearing different faces.

The Watchers and Their Fall

To understand where demons come from—and why the world suffers—
we turn to one of the most haunting and powerful stories outside the
biblical canon: the tale of the Watchers, as told in the Book of 1 Enoch.

This ancient text, part of the pseudepigrapha—writings attributed to
biblical figures but excluded from official scripture—offers a mythic origin
for evil itself. It tells of divine beings, angels called the Watchers, who
were sent to Earth not to destroy, but to watch. They came as guardians,
emissaries of divine order. But they did not remain that way for long.

Led by Azazel, or Semyaza, the Watchers broke their oath. They fell not
through pride alone, but through desire. They took human lovers, shared
forbidden knowledge, and fathered the Nephilim: giants, fierce and
monstrous, who brought chaos and destruction to the world. Their
presence defiled the Earth, and their teachings—warfare, enchantments,
sorcery, cosmetics, metallurgy—were deemed corrupting and dangerous.

In the myth, this rebellion shatters the balance. The Watchers' fall marks
a turning point: the moment when sin enters the world not by human
fault, but through the mingling of the divine and the mortal. The Nephilim
are eventually destroyed in a great purge, but their spirits remain.
Rootless, restless, and denied passage to the heavens or underworld, they
become the first demons—disembodied, angry, and unbound.

The tale is often framed as a warning against seeking forbidden
knowledge or defying divine law. But for modern readers—especially
those of us who walk magical or liminal paths—it raises deeper questions.
What is the cost of wisdom? Who decides what knowledge is forbidden?

And what happens when divine beings choose to stand beside humanity, even if it damns them?

After their rebellion, the Watchers were not simply banished—they were bound. According to *1 Enoch*, God commanded the archangels Michael and Gabriel to cast them into the abyss—a prison of darkness where they would remain until the final judgment. Chapter 10 offers a vivid image: these once-radiant beings, now fallen, chained beneath the earth, sealed away in silence and shadow.

But their punishment doesn't strip them of all purpose. In a strange turn, the fallen ones still serve a role in the divine plan. They become instruments of judgment—tormentors, yes, but also enforcers of divine justice. This duality—that demons can be both destroyers and tools of a greater order—would echo through Christian theology for centuries. It paved the way for later ideas about Satan, fallen angels, and the cosmic drama between light and darkness.

It's important to remember *when* this story was written. The Book of 1 Enoch emerged during a time of deep turmoil for the Jewish people, likely around the 3rd century BCE. Pressured by foreign empires and struggling to maintain cultural identity, these stories weren't just myth—they were reassurance. The Watchers' fall became a promise: the corrupt would be punished. The faithful would endure. And no matter how chaotic the world became, justice was coming.

1 Enoch is more than a tale of rebellion. It's a meditation on suffering, injustice, and the unseen forces that shape our world. It asks: Why do the wicked prosper? Where does evil come from—and where does it go when the gods stop watching?

Though not included in the official canon, *1 Enoch* deeply influenced early Christian thought. Church fathers turned to its visions to understand the roots of sin, the fall of angels, and the war between heaven and hell. The story of the Watchers became the soil from which Christian demonology would grow—shaping how we view demons, spiritual warfare, and the ultimate reckoning to come.

2. THE FIRST REBEL

Among the figures of early demonology, few stand out like Azazel. His story is more than just a cautionary tale—it is the blueprint of rebellion, the spark that set divine disobedience into motion. Woven through ancient texts and whispered across generations, Azazel embodies the sacred tension between wisdom and transgression.

His most well-known appearance is in the *Book of Enoch*, within the section known as the *Book of the Watchers*. Here, Azazel is named as one angel who descended to Earth to offer forbidden knowledge. He teaches humanity the art of warfare, metallurgy, ornamentation, and cosmetics. Skills of survival and seduction. Power and beauty. And in doing so, he opens a door that was meant to stay closed.

It's not merely his descent that damns him, but the corruption he brings. According to *1 Enoch 10:4–6*, Azazel is bound and cast into a shadowed abyss—a divine prison where he remains, waiting for final judgment. His fate mirrors that of Prometheus, Loki, and other mythic transgressors: punished not only for defying the gods, but for giving dangerous gifts to humankind.

Azazel becomes the archetype of the celestial rebel—the one who crosses the threshold, who challenges the divine order by empowering mortals. In this way, he is a forerunner to later figures like Satan in Christian theology. But while Satan is often framed as the adversary, Azazel's rebellion feels more complex. He is a teacher. A tempter. A being who sees potential in humanity and is willing to risk everything to awaken it.

Over time, Azazel's image shifted. In apocryphal Jewish texts and early Christian writings, his actions became symbols of ambition, hubris, and the human desire to reach beyond prescribed limits. His punishment serves as a cosmic warning: there is a price for reaching into the fire of divine knowledge.

Yet Azazel's roots dig deeper than Enoch. Some scholars link him to Azazil, a figure from Ugaritic lore associated with defiance against the divine will. Others point to even broader Ancient Near Eastern influences—where gods and semi-divine beings challenge the established order by sharing forbidden truths. In Canaanite and Babylonian myth, these themes repeat: transgression, revelation, and punishment.

Azazel's myth also echoes the chaos figures of Mesopotamian stories— like Tiamat, who rises against the younger gods and is torn apart in a cosmic war. But where Tiamat embodies primordial chaos, Azazel's rebellion is intellectual, cultural. His crime is knowledge. And that's what makes him so powerful, and so dangerous to some. He is not just a demon—he is a mirror. A symbol of the seeker's dilemma: to stay obedient in the light, or reach into the shadow and find something older, wilder, and far less comfortable.

His fall marked more than a celestial rebellion—it became a symbol of dangerous enlightenment, the price of transgressing divine law.

Yet within this myth lies a paradox. Azazel is both corrupter and catalyst. A bringer of chaos, yes—but also a bearer of wisdom. In this, he reflects a powerful archetype: the rebellious teacher, the one who dares to give humanity the tools the gods would keep hidden. This theme echoes in other traditions—Prometheus stealing fire, Lucifer bringing light.

In modern magical practice, Azazel is often honored as a patron of transformation. Practitioners within paths like Luciferianism and demonolatry see him not as a being of malevolence, but of empowerment. He represents the pursuit of hidden truths, personal sovereignty, and the courage to challenge imposed order.

Authors like Michael W. Ford have portrayed Azazel as a symbol of liberation—an initiator who guides the practitioner through the fires of knowledge and into self-realization.

Mainstream Abrahamic traditions, however, frame Azazel quite differently. He is seen as a corrupter, a demonic presence responsible for spiritual decay. His name is often equated with Satan or with the wilderness demon to whom the scapegoat was sent during the Yom Kippur ritual (Leviticus 16). In this rite, a goat bearing the sins of the people was cast into the wild "to Azazel"—a powerful metaphor of exile, impurity, and divine rejection. Whether Azazel in this context refers to a literal being or a desolate place remains debated, but the symbolism is potent: he becomes the vessel for what is cast out.

For many demonolaters, exploring Azazel's origins is both frustrating and exhilarating. The lack of definitive historical sources means much of his identity must be pieced together—through ancient texts, mythological parallels, and personal gnosis. Was he once a forgotten god? A localized spirit later demonized under monotheism? We may never know for certain.

Some traditions suggest links between Azazel and other ancient figures like the Sumerian god Utu or even the Assyrian deity Ashur. These comparisons draw on shared themes—light, knowledge, authority, and landscape—but lack strong historical evidence. They are speculative, symbolic associations rather than proven connections. For the purposes of this book, such parallels are acknowledged but not emphasized. Azazel stands powerfully on his own.

Ultimately, what matters is not just who Azazel was, but who he is now—how his myth speaks to us in this time, and how we as practitioners relate to him. To some, he is a guide through the wilderness. To others, a tempter at the edge of forbidden truths. But always, he is a figure who invites us to ask the dangerous questions—and to bear the weight of the answers

Who was the first rebel?

Across spiritual traditions, one question continues to echo: *Who was the first to defy the divine?* In Christian theology, the answer is often Lucifer—the light-bringer cast down for his pride. This belief draws from interpretations of Isaiah 14:12–15 and Ezekiel 28:12–17. Though originally written about the kings of Babylon and Tyre, these passages were later reimagined to describe a celestial fall. Over time, Lucifer became synonymous with Satan, the adversary, the original rebel who sought to rise above God—and was cast down for it.

Literature like John Milton's *Paradise Lost* entrenched this image: Lucifer as the proud archangel leading a cosmic revolt, reshaping Heaven and Hell in his wake.

But Christian tradition is not the only one to tell the story of rebellion. In *The Book of Enoch*, Azazel plays a different role. As one of the Watchers—angels sent to guide humanity—he descended to Earth and broke divine law by taking human wives and teaching forbidden knowledge: metallurgy, magic, weaponry. His transgression was not driven by pride, but by contact, intimacy, interference. Azazel did not seek to dethrone the divine, but to empower humanity—an act with unintended consequences.

Where Lucifer's rebellion is cosmic and symbolic, Azazel's is terrestrial and cultural. Lucifer challenges the throne of Heaven; Azazel corrupts the world of mortals. One shakes the heavens, the other changes the Earth. Yet both reflect archetypes of transgression—figures who cross boundaries, awaken change, and suffer for it.

And they are not alone. In Jewish mysticism, Samael—the angel of death and accuser—is another liminal figure. Some traditions link him to the serpent in Eden, tempting Eve and unsettling divine order. In Islamic tradition, Iblis refuses Allah's command to bow to Adam, claiming superiority as a being of smokeless fire. His fall mirrors Lucifer's: pride, disobedience, and exile.

Beyond the Abrahamic traditions, we find Prometheus—the Titan who stole fire from Olympus to gift to humankind. His rebellion, born of compassion rather than pride, brought illumination but also punishment. Chained for eternity, he became an enduring symbol of sacrifice and the cost of forbidden knowledge.

Figures like Lilith, said to be Adam's first wife in Jewish folklore, also embody this archetype. She refused to submit, fled Eden, and was demonized for her independence. Her story, like Azazel's, speaks not of war against Heaven, but of resistance to imposed order—especially patriarchal control.

Even in mythologies far from the biblical world, the rebel appears. In Hindu cosmology, the Asuras rise against the Devas in cycles of conflict and balance. In Egyptian myth, Set kills his brother Osiris, disrupting the cosmic harmony. In Jewish legend, Rahab, a primordial sea serpent, resists God's act of creation and is defeated—another chaos-being silenced by order.

These stories, scattered across cultures, point to something deeper than doctrine. The rebel—whether angel, demon, god, or titan—is not always a villain. Sometimes they are challengers, teachers, liberators. Sometimes they fall because they dare to act. And sometimes, they fall because they must.

Lucifer and Azazel may stand at the center of Judeo-Christian frameworks, but the archetype of rebellion is older, broader, and far more complex. It reflects humanity's deep, enduring tension between obedience and autonomy. Between divine order and personal will. Between the heavens above—and the fire we choose to carry.

The Importance of Understanding History

For those of us walking occult, esoteric, or spiritual paths, understanding the lore of demonic entities is far more than an academic pursuit—it is a vital part of our work. These beings are not mere symbols confined to dusty texts; they live at the crossroads of myth, mystery, and magic. To engage with them fully, we must know where they come from, how they were shaped, and how they continue to evolve within the human psyche and spiritual tradition.

Entities like Azazel hold deep archetypal resonance. His story is not just one of rebellion, but of transformation. He teaches forbidden knowledge, walks the boundaries between worlds, and becomes a guide for those seeking to break free of imposed structures. For many practitioners, working with Azazel means facing the self—its shadows, its hunger for truth, its longing for freedom. To understand his history is to understand our own potential for becoming.

When we approach these spirits—especially those with layered and controversial pasts—we must do so with knowledge, reverence, and clarity. Misunderstanding or oversimplifying a being like Azazel risks flattening his presence into stereotype. But when we study his origins, we step into relationship with him. We recognize how cultural fears, religious agendas, and evolving mythologies have shaped how we see him today— and how we might choose to see him differently.

This awareness doesn't just deepen our understanding. It empowers our practice. Whether in ritual, meditation, or invocation, knowing a spirit's history allows us to engage more intentionally. Azazel's associations— metallurgy, war, ornamentation, divination—aren't just mythic flourishes. They are doorways. Pathways into personal ritual and direct experience.

By aligning our work with these domains, we create space for authentic connection.

Azazel's mythos is rich with themes of adversity, enlightenment, and the sacred fire of rebellion. These are not just ancient stories. They are mirrors. They reflect the journey of the practitioner—the struggle to shed imposed limits, the choice to walk an untamed path, and the courage it takes to evolve.

At the end of this book, we will move from history into praxis—exploring how to work with spirits like Azazel respectfully, powerfully, and with a clear understanding of their depth.

3. From Goddesses to Shadows—The Transformation of Deities

In the chapters before, we explored how gods were cast down, renamed, or recast as demons as monotheism spread and older belief systems were dismantled. Now, we return to those themes—but with a sharper focus.

This chapter turns its gaze toward the feminine divine. Toward goddesses who once held dominion over love, war, birth, death, and desire—and how their power was split, vilified, and ultimately hidden behind masks of shadow. Figures like Ishtar and Lilith are not merely survivors of this transformation—they are symbols of what was lost and what remains.

Their stories are more than myth. They speak to the suppression of feminine sovereignty, to the fear of autonomy and sensuality, and to the persistence of divine power, even when buried beneath centuries of cultural shame and theological revision. To understand their fall is to begin reclaiming what they represent: unbroken, untamed, and still burning in the dark.

In the shifting sands of the ancient Near East, two powerful figures emerged—goddesses who defied the expectations of their time, embodying both the nurturing and destructive forces of the universe.

One was Ishtar, radiant and tempestuous, goddess of love, war, and fertility, worshipped across the fertile crescent as both creator and destroyer. The other was Lilith, a shadowed, rebellious presence whispered through myth and folklore, a spirit tied to seduction, wilderness, and the primal dark.

Though separated by geography and myth, these two figures share an uncanny resonance. Their stories spiral around common themes: sovereignty, rebellion, transformation, and the feminine divine in its rawest form. They were more than goddesses—they were forces of nature. Uncompromising. Untamed.

In Mesopotamia, Ishtar's myths burn like fire. She ruled the domains of sex and war, love and vengeance, life and death. In *The Descent of Inanna*, she passes through the seven gates of the underworld, each one stripping her of power, until she stands naked before death itself. Her journey is not a fall, but a confrontation—a ritual of rebirth, a reclaiming of divine sovereignty in a world that demands submission. Even in the *Epic of Gilgamesh*, her divine pride refuses humiliation. When rejected, she unleashes the Bull of Heaven—not as punishment, but as proof that even gods bleed passion.

And then, there is Lilith. Not born of rib, but of earth. Not made to submit, but to stand equal. In early Jewish lore, she is Adam's first wife— the one who refused to lie beneath him. When forced to choose between obedience and exile, she chose the wild. In the eyes of later tradition, that choice made her monstrous. A seductress. A child-killer. A demoness. But in truth, Lilith's exile was an act of radical self-sovereignty.

Unlike Ishtar, whose divine status was eroded over time, Lilith's divinity was never allowed to fully take root. She was born in the margins—at the edges of gardens, temples, and laws. Yet she, too, descended—not into the underworld, but into mythic shadow. Where Ishtar passed through gates, Lilith fled through them, unrepentant and unbroken.

As monotheism rose, both figures were transformed. Ishtar's sensuality became sin; her strength, hubris. Her divine rage, once sacred, was cast as chaos. Lilith, once a possible goddess of fertility and the night, became the "mother of demons" in Jewish folklore. Texts like *The Alphabet of Ben Sira* gave her a name and a lineage—birthing demonic offspring, seducing men in their sleep, stealing children from cradles. The wild feminine became something to fear. To silence.

Both Ishtar and Lilith walk the boundaries—between divinity and demonhood, autonomy and punishment, reverence and repression. Their connection to the dark is not accidental. Ishtar's descent into the underworld mirrors Lilith's retreat into wilderness and night. Each of them enters the places society fears. And each returns—not as victim, but as something transformed.

To study these women is to confront a truth that patriarchal systems have long tried to erase: that feminine power is not meant to be tamed. It births and destroys. It nurtures and challenges. It seduces and demands.

To stand before Ishtar is to face the storm and the stillness, the lover and the warrior, the blood-soaked battlefield and the fragrant bed. She does not ask to be understood—only to be honored in her fullness. The ancients didn't flinch from her duality. They knew that love without rage is weak, and creation without destruction is incomplete. In stories passed down through stone tablets and temple hymns, Ishtar was not "balanced" in the way modern sensibilities might demand. She was volatile. Passionate. Divine in her contradictions.

In *The Descent of Inanna*, she strips herself bare—of titles, jewels, power—passing through the seven gates of the underworld not in shame, but in purpose. Her journey is not a fall; it is a rite. A breaking open. A remembering of death's place in the cycle of rebirth. She becomes queen of shadow and light. And in doing so, claims dominion over both.

In *The Epic of Gilgamesh*, we see how easily that power threatens the pride of men. When she is rejected, she answers not with silence, but with the Bull of Heaven. Her wrath is divine, not petty. To the people of her time, this was not excess—it was justice.

But later ages were less kind. The rising tides of monotheism demanded order, obedience, and control—qualities she did not possess and never desired. Her sensuality became seduction. Her sacred rage became chaos. Her name, once invoked with reverence, faded into warning.

Yet for those who walk the crooked path, she has never been gone. Ishtar remains the guardian of thresholds between life and death, rage and desire, power and vulnerability. She speaks to those of us who are tired of being told we must be only one thing. She whispers to the parts of us that long to descend, to rage, to rise again—not clean, but whole. To work with Ishtar is to embrace discomfort. To honor her is to stand in the fire of your own becoming.

Lilith lives on the edges—of myth, of memory, of every story we were told to forget. Where Ishtar ruled from temples and thundered across battlefields, Lilith whispered through cracks in the walls, through the wind in the desert, through the cries of women left unheard.

She was never tamed, never worshipped in the same grand way—but her power has endured, dark and feral and free.

In Kabbalistic tradition, Lilith is woven into the shadows of the *Sitra Achra*—the "Other Side," the realm of chaos, impurity, and divine inversion. Here, she is paired with Samael, the archangel of death, not in submission, but as a consort. Their union is one of mirrored power— feminine and masculine forces outside divine law, birthing a lineage not of angels, but of demons.

Though she appears only briefly in early Jewish texts, Lilith's myth grew over centuries. The *Talmud* and *Midrash* reference her as a demon of the night, a threat to women in childbirth, a stealer of infants. Her name became a warning. Her presence, something to fear. But beneath the layers of superstition and patriarchal anxiety, another truth pulses: Lilith is what cannot be controlled.

Over time, this fear became fascination. In *The Alphabet of Ben Sira*, a medieval Jewish text, Lilith is named explicitly as Adam's first wife—a being made of the same earth, not bone, who refused to submit. When she demanded equality and was denied it, she spoke the unspeakable Name and fled Eden. That act of defiance sealed her fate—and secured her immortality.

In modern occult traditions, Lilith is no longer simply a demon. She is a symbol of sovereignty. Of refusal. Of sexual power unshamed. She is the mother of demons, not because she is evil, but because she births what the world cannot accept. Rebellion. Desire. Wild wisdom. Shadow truths.

To some, she is a goddess in her own right—a dark mother, a protectress of the exiled, a guide through the liminal. She does not demand worship. She invites understanding. And that invitation is not always gentle. Even in popular culture—books, films, television—Lilith has returned, crowned as the matriarch of rebellion. Often cast as the "mother of demons," her image still disturbs. Still entices. Still resists. And perhaps that is her most enduring legacy. While others were cast down, Lilith was never caught. She fled to the wilderness and made it hers. And from there, she continues to call to those who cannot breathe within the walls of obedience.

Ishtar and Lilith were not alone in their descent into shadow. Across lands and cultures, gods who once walked the earth as embodiments of love, death, war, and wisdom were pulled from their thrones and cast into silence. With the rise of monotheistic empires, the ancient world's pantheons began to fracture. Some gods were absorbed, reshaped, or quietly faded into myth. Others were actively demonized—turned into symbols of sin, rebellion, and danger.

In Egypt, gods like Ra, Osiris, and Set once defined cosmic balance. Set, in particular, began as a powerful force of chaos and strength—a necessary counterpart to order, and protector of the sun god Ra through the underworld. But as Christianity spread through Egypt, Set's darker traits became dominant in the public imagination. No longer seen as a balancing force, he became a figure of malevolence and destruction. Chaos, once a sacred force in the cycle of renewal, was now equated with evil.

Osiris, god of the afterlife and rebirth, fared better—yet even his story was diminished. His dominion over death and resurrection clashed with new doctrines of eternal salvation through a singular god. The eternal cycle he represented was replaced with linear judgment. His myth, once central to Egyptian identity, was reinterpreted or forgotten.

To the north, in Greece, the gods suffered a similar fate. Hades, who ruled the underworld with solemn justice, was reimagined as the ruler of Hell. His neutral governance of the dead was rewritten into eternal punishment.

Pan, god of the wild, the erotic, and the untamed, became the template for Satan himself—his goat legs and horned crown transformed from symbols of nature and fertility into icons of wickedness and temptation. And Ares, god of war, once honored for his brutal honesty in embodying conflict, became a demon of destruction in the eyes of the new faith.

This wasn't simply mythology fading—it was a rewriting of power. As monotheism expanded, the gods of old were painted as obstacles to salvation. Where once there were many faces of the divine—divinities who reflected the full spectrum of human experience—now there could be only one god, and all others were false, fallen, or demonic.

But not all gods were treated equally in this transformation. The gods of Greece, Rome, and Egypt were, over time, recast as myth. As Western culture secularized, these deities found new life in poetry, art, and philosophy. They became cultural symbols—Hercules a hero, Venus a muse, Athena an icon of wisdom. Their divinity was stripped, but their stories endured.

The gods and spirits of the Ancient Near East, however, were not afforded such mercy. Deities like Baal, Astarte, and Asmodeus were woven into the scriptures of monotheistic religions—not as misunderstood gods, but as demons. These names became curses. These figures, who once ruled over storms, fertility, wisdom, and justice, were bound into roles of pure opposition. The sacred complexity of their nature was erased. No mythology, no allegory—just evil.

Where Pan became a metaphor and Horus a symbol, Baal remained a warning. Astarte became a temptress. Asmodeus, a devil. Their transformation was not poetic—it was theological warfare.

This difference matters. It shows us which stories we have been allowed to reclaim—and which still remain imprisoned beneath the weight of dogma. The gods of the ANE are still buried beneath fear. Still seen as threats, not teachers. Still cast as demons, not divinities in exile. And yet, they persist. In whispers. In names. In dreams. Waiting, like Lilith and Ishtar, for those willing to look deeper. To unearth what was buried. To remember what was made to be forgotten.

Naamah (sometimes spelled Na'amah or Na'mah) appears in various Jewish mystical, folkloric, and occult texts. Her name means *"pleasant"* or *"beautiful"* in Hebrew, but despite that, she's often portrayed as a dangerous and seductive figure in later demonological traditions.

In Kabbalistic tradition, Naamah becomes one of the four "Queens of the Demons" or "wives of Samael," alongside Lilith, Agrat bat Mahlat, and Eisheth Zenunim. These four demonesses are seen as the personifications of lust, seduction, and spiritual corruption, often linked to the *qliphoth* — the shadow or "shell" side of the Tree of Life.

Naamah is often specifically associated with seduction and prostitution. She's said to tempt men in their sleep, cause nocturnal emissions, and draw their vitality away. In some versions, she also has a role in harming children or spreading disease, like Lilith.

Artwork of Queen Naamah by Emmy Sollien©2023

4. The Origin Of Satan

Before he was the Devil, Satan was a whisper. A question. A test. He walked not as an enemy of God, but as part of heaven's own court—an adversary, not a traitor.

In the Hebrew Bible, ha-satan means "the accuser," a title, not a name. He appears as a divine prosecutor, a being who challenges human righteousness and exposes hypocrisy—not out of malice, but as part of a cosmic order. In Job, he walks among the divine council, questioning the integrity of God's creation. In Zechariah, he stands beside the high priest Joshua, an accuser in the divine court. There is no pitchfork, no flames—only scrutiny. Only a role.

And yet, the world was changing. The people who wrote these stories were exiles, survivors, subjects of empires. They had tasted injustice, seen temples burn, and wrestled with questions no orderly theology could answer. Why do the wicked thrive? Why do the righteous suffer? Where is God when the world falls apart?

Into this chaos, Satan began to transform. Apocalyptic texts such as 1 Enoch laid the groundwork for a new narrative: one where heavenly beings could fall, rebel, and corrupt.

The Watchers, those angels who descended and broke divine law, became a prototype. Pride, forbidden knowledge, transgression—they were no longer divine quirks, but sins with consequences.

And somewhere in the background, the Adversary took shape—not as a test, but as a threat.

By the time Christian theology emerged, Satan had shifted from divine accuser to cosmic rebel. Passages in Isaiah 14 and Ezekiel 28, once addressed to human kings, were now read as metaphors for his fall. The "morning star," who sought to raise his throne above the heavens, became the Devil. The dragon of Revelation was cast from heaven. A war had begun, and Satan now stood on the far side of the battlefield.

But this fall wasn't only spiritual—it was strategic. Monotheism required opposition. If there was only one God, then evil needed a source outside Him. The human tendency to doubt, desire, or disobey had to come from somewhere. And so, Satan became not just a being—but a container. A name for every question religion couldn't answer. A scapegoat for the shadow of the divine. He became pride, lust, rebellion, suffering, temptation. He became the dark mirror.

As Christianity grew, so too did the need for a clear line between light and darkness. The fluid cosmologies of older traditions—where gods could be both generous and wrathful, where chaos had its place—were no longer sufficient. The new order demanded purity. Obedience. A singular divine will. But human nature is rarely so clean.

Satan became the one who blurred the edges. The one who whispered in gardens, who tempted in deserts, who led angels into rebellion and humans into ruin.

Christian thinkers like St. Augustine codified his fall: pride had driven him to challenge God, ambition had made him reach too high, and now he was cast down, twisted into the ruler of all things wicked. No longer a function of divine justice—he was the enemy of heaven.

And so the Devil was born.

His origin was patchwork—a blend of scripture, apocrypha, fear, and necessity. Passages originally written about tyrant kings were reinterpreted as metaphors for celestial treason. Jewish apocalyptic visions of fallen angels were woven into a Christian framework of salvation and damnation. Where the Watchers had once been punished for defying divine law, Satan was now the architect of all defiance.

By the time Revelation was written, Satan stood fully formed as the great adversary. The red dragon, hurled from heaven, now ruled the earth with deception and rage, waging war against God's people. His story echoed older myths—the serpent gods of Mesopotamia, the chaos monsters of Canaan—but now he was permanent. Fixed. No longer a part of the divine order, but the antithesis of it. Dualism had arrived. And it was absolute. The world, once held in balance by gods like Ishtar or Set—who embodied both creation and destruction—was now split. Good and evil. God and Satan. Heaven and Hell. The ambiguity that had once defined the sacred was replaced with moral clarity enforced by fear.

But dualism is not just theology—it is control. And Satan, ever the rebel, became the embodiment of everything that could not be controlled.

In time, Satan came to embody not just evil, but rebellion itself. He was no longer just a tempter or a deceiver—he was the voice of the forbidden. The flame of desire. The will to say no. And this made him dangerous—not just to heaven, but to any system built on obedience.

To cast Satan as the ruler of Hell, the torturer of souls, was to cement him in the role of divine punishment. But to see him as the rebel who would rather reign in Hell than serve in Heaven—as Milton did in Paradise Lost— was to flirt with something deeper. Something human.

In many ways, Satan's myth is not about a being—it is about a boundary. Between what we are told is right, and what we truly want. Between obedience and autonomy. Between the divine and the forbidden. And so, over time, Satan became more than the Christian Devil. He became a mirror to the soul.

Modern Satanism, Occultism, and the Flame of the Self

As centuries passed, the terror surrounding Satan began to shift. Not disappear—but shift. In the shadow of fire-and-brimstone sermons, a quiet revolution began: some no longer saw Satan as a monster, but as a mirror. A question. A choice.

In the 20th century, figures like Anton LaVey gave form to that whispering defiance. His Church of Satan, founded in 1966, was not a religion in the traditional sense—but a declaration of war against religious conformity. LaVeyan Satanism is atheistic, using Satan not as a literal being but as a symbol: of indulgence, pride, and personal empowerment. A rebel god for a world that no longer feared the old one.

Here, Satan became a mask of freedom—a ritualized "yes" to the self, and a "no" to guilt. Where once the Adversary was cast out for pride, now that same pride was celebrated. Rebellion became virtue. Knowledge was no longer forbidden—it was holy.

Then came The Satanic Temple, a 21st-century evolution: part protest, part performance, part spiritual philosophy. They used Satanic imagery to challenge political theocracy, defend bodily autonomy, and reclaim religious freedom. Their Satan is a trickster, a liberator, a figure who refuses to bow. He is not evil, but resistance personified.

In these movements, Satan is no longer the enemy of God—he is the enemy of tyranny. Not a corrupter of souls, but a defender of individual will.

Outside organized Satanism, Luciferianism emerged as a distinct path: not about opposition, but illumination. Here, Satan (or Lucifer) is not a destroyer—but a teacher. A bearer of light. The Promethean fire-bringer who dares to awaken humanity, even at great cost. In this current, Satan is less the Christian devil and more the archetype of forbidden wisdom. He is the one who hands you the book, opens the door, lights the match.

Occult traditions often link him to the pursuit of personal mastery—working through the shadow, facing fear, integrating the self. He becomes not just an adversary, but an initiator. The one who tests, who breaks illusions, who strips away comfort so that transformation may occur.

In Demonolatry, practitioners may honor Satan as a central figure—not as a destroyer of worlds, but as a primal force of will, drive, and sovereignty. His presence is often invoked in ritual not with fear, but with reverence. Through offerings, sigils, and sacred names, Satan becomes a guide—not to darkness for its own sake, but to the power that lies within it.

Not everyone who sees Satan sees a spirit. For some, he is psychological—a Jungian shadow. A mirror of our suppressed desires, our rage, our lust, our hunger for freedom. In this frame, to "meet the Devil" is to confront the parts of the self we have been told to fear. And to integrate him is to stop running from ourselves. This Satan does not tempt. He invites. He says: Look deeper. Do not avert your gaze. What you have called evil may be power. What you have feared in yourself may be a gate.

The Satan of today wears many faces. To some, he is still the adversary—the enemy of the divine. But to others, he is a path. A force. A name for the spark inside us that refuses to kneel. Like Lilith, he is the one who left paradise rather than submit. Like Ishtar, he descends into shadow, transforms, and rises changed. Like the gods of old, he was dethroned not because he was weak—but because he was powerful.

In demonology, we must ask not just who these beings are—but who they became, and why. Satan is not just the Christian Devil. He is a figure shaped by exile, rebellion, fear, and reclamation. He is a vessel for what society condemns—and what the soul still seeks. To study him is not to worship him, but to confront the deeper question: What part of the divine was cast out so that order might rule? And what power still waits in the wilderness to be remembered?

Lucifer – The Morning Star and the Rebel Flame

He fell, not with a scream, but with brilliance. Before his name became a warning, it was a title of praise. Lucifer, the light-bringer. The morning star. The herald of dawn. His story is one of brilliance turned to shadow—of reverence transformed into rebellion. The word lucifer appears only once in the Latin Vulgate Bible, in Isaiah 14:12:

"How you have fallen from heaven, O morning star, son of the dawn."

This passage originally described the downfall of a Babylonian king—one who dared rise too high. But the symbolism was too rich, too potent. Over time, tradition transfigured this fallen star into a heavenly being cast down for pride. And thus, Lucifer was born—not just as a poetic metaphor, but as a celestial rebel, exiled for daring to shine too brightly.

Later, in the hands of Christian theologians and poets, Lucifer took on flesh and fire. In John Milton's Paradise Lost, he becomes a tragic antihero—charismatic, proud, and defiant. He challenges the divine order not for evil's sake, but for the right to choose.

"Better to reign in Hell than serve in Heaven."

Milton did not invent Lucifer, but he gave him a voice—and through that voice, he became a symbol. Not of sin, but of sovereignty.

Lucifer's rebellion has echoed ever since—not just through churches and cathedrals, but through philosophy, literature, and magic. He is more than a fallen angel. He is the eternal question: What if I refuse to kneel?

To fall is not always to fail. In Lucifer's descent, many found not damnation, but illumination. Enlightenment thinkers, poets, and occultists looked past the fear and fire—and saw a figure who dared to ask questions. Who refused blind obedience. Who reached for knowledge, even when it burned.

In Gnostic traditions, this Light-Bringer is not a villain but a liberator. Gnostics believed the world was a prison built by a lesser god—a demiurge who cloaked ignorance in divine authority. To escape this world, one needed gnosis, hidden knowledge. And who better to deliver it than the one cast down for seeking it? In this vision, Lucifer becomes not the enemy of humanity, but its ally. A guide through illusion. A bearer of forbidden truths. His flame is not a destructive fire—but a lantern in the dark.

In the realm of modern Luciferianism, he is not worshipped as a god, but embraced as an archetype—a symbol of sovereignty, inner strength, and the pursuit of personal truth. Writers like Michael W. Ford and others have expanded on Lucifer's role not as a deceiver, but a teacher. A mentor of transformation. A force that challenges the initiate to confront fear, shed ignorance, and emerge reborn. In The Devil's Bible and similar texts, Lucifer is cast not as a tyrant, but as a mirror to one's own divine spark. Luciferianism is not about indulgence for its own sake, nor rebellion without purpose. It is a path of self-mastery. It embraces the flame of will, the wisdom of shadow, and the power of claiming one's own name in a world of imposed identities.

Where Satan represents opposition, Lucifer represents liberation. In recent decades, the cultural veil over Lucifer has thinned. He appears now in books, comics, music, and television—not always as the villain, but as something more human. More complex. In Neil Gaiman's Sandman, the Morningstar leaves Hell not to torment—but to be free. He walks among mortals, searching for meaning, seeking to define himself outside the role the universe assigned him. In shows like Lucifer or Supernatural, he is charming, flawed, witty, defiant—a figure struggling with identity, destiny, and redemption. The Devil no longer hides in the shadows. He stands in the light, asking us to see beyond the fear. And in doing so, he becomes what he always was: a reflection.

In some Demonolatry and esoteric traditions, Lucifer is honored through rituals of transformation. Not as a fallen deity to be appeased, but as a force to invoke when seeking clarity, empowerment, or rebirth.

He is called upon during moments of personal crisis or awakening—when old beliefs crumble and something new must rise in their place. His presence is often felt in initiatory rites, dreamwork, or pathworkings through the shadow. Where his light shines, it does not soothe—it exposes. It strips away illusion, burns through falsehood, and demands authenticity.

To walk with Lucifer is to step into sovereignty. Lucifer's story is not one of simple rebellion. It is the story of what happens when a being dares to ask why. Why serve without question? Why accept the world as it is? Why not reach for more—even if it means falling? To some, this is arrogance. To others, it is courage.

Lucifer's flame continues to burn—not in the pits of Hell, but in the hearts of those who seek truth on their own terms. He stands alongside Lilith, Azazel, and the Watchers—those cast out, not for wickedness, but for daring to transgress divine law. For seeking knowledge, power, or love beyond what was allowed.

In this light, Lucifer is not the enemy. He is the invitation. To think. To challenge. To become.

5. The Concept of Hell — A Journey Through Fire and Darkness

Beneath the earth, beyond the veil, or deep within the human psyche—Hell has always lurked in the spaces where fear, judgment, and mystery converge. No single vision defines it. Across time and cultures, Hell has taken many forms: a desolate underworld, a prison of ice, a furnace of divine wrath, a realm of shadow, a mirror of guilt. It is both myth and metaphor. It burns in scripture and flickers in the subconscious. It punishes. It transforms. It waits.

Long before monotheistic religions drew sharp lines between good and evil, ancient peoples imagined the afterlife not as a moral courtroom, but as a continuation of existence. In the clay tablets of Mesopotamia, the dead wandered the dust-choked corridors of Irkalla, a bleak and joyless land ruled by Ereshkigal, Queen of the Underworld. There was no reward or punishment—only stillness, and the dim echo of a life left behind.

In Egypt, the dead stood trial. Their hearts weighed against the feather of Ma'at, goddess of truth and balance. Those found wanting were devoured, not eternally punished, but annihilated—erased from cosmic memory. In Greece, the afterlife fractured into realms: the peaceful Elysian Fields, the solemn Asphodel Meadows, and the torment of Tartarus. The soul's fate mirrored its deeds. The gods did not offer redemption, only consequences. The Norse spoke of Helheim, the cold realm of the forgotten dead. Not for the wicked—simply for those who did not die with valor. Hel, its ruler, bore a face half-beautiful, half-rotted: a goddess of dualities. Her realm was not cruel, only inevitable. These early hells were not places of eternal moral punishment, but realms of death's shadow. They held no fire. Only silence, cold, or grey forgetfulness.

The rise of monotheism brought a dramatic shift—not just in how gods were worshipped, but in how death was understood. A new binary emerged: heaven or hell, reward or punishment. The grey became black and white.

In early Jewish texts, the realm of the dead was known as Sheol—a dark, quiet place beneath the earth where all souls, righteous or wicked, returned. It was not a place of fire or retribution, but of shadow and stillness. There was no judgment yet—only waiting.

But in the intertestamental period, under the influence of Persian dualism and Hellenistic thought, the afterlife began to divide. The wicked now had a place apart. The faithful had hope of paradise. In apocalyptic writings like Daniel and 1 Enoch, the seeds of judgment were planted—and with them, the fires began to flicker.

By the time of Christianity, those flames had become central. Gehenna—a real valley outside Jerusalem once associated with sacrifice and waste— was transformed in the New Testament into a symbol of divine punishment. No longer a pit for refuse, it became the place where the wicked would burn eternally. Hades, borrowed from Greek cosmology, became synonymous with Hell itself. And Satan, once a shadowy accuser, now stood as its ruler. It was the theologians—Augustine, Tertullian, Aquinas—who sculpted Hell into something enduring and exacting.

It was divine justice, perfect and irreversible. Fire that never ceased. Pain without mercy. Separation from God not for a time, but forever.

And then came the poets. In Dante Alighieri's Inferno, Hell was given structure, form, and horror. Nine circles spiraling downward, each more terrible than the last. A Hell for liars. A Hell for traitors. A Hell for the unrepentant lovers of pleasure. Dante's vision became doctrine. His imagination, lit by medieval anxieties, drew the map that countless would follow.

In Islam, the fire burned just as hot—but with a different purpose. Jahannam, the Qur'anic hell, is a place of blazing torment and searing heat, described in vivid language and layered with meaning. It is the destiny of those who reject the will of Allah, the wicked, and the arrogant. Yet even here, there is nuance. Unlike the eternal damnation of Christian Hell, some souls may be purified in Jahannam and released through Allah's mercy. The Qur'an speaks not only of fire, but of justice— measured, precise, and divinely balanced. There are seven levels of Hell, each reflecting the severity of one's choices. No soul suffers more than it deserves. And no one is beyond redemption, should God will it.

In this vision, Hell is not chaos. It is order—the cleansing fire of divine law. In the modern age, fire gave way to metaphor. As belief systems shifted and the authority of religious institutions waned, Hell began to retreat— from the realm of the afterlife into the human mind.

Sigmund Freud called it repression. A war between desire and morality. The id and the superego locked in a private Gehenna. Carl Jung gave it form: the Shadow—that part of the self buried deep, made of shame, rage, and unlived truths.

To descend into one's shadow was to walk through a personal hell. But unlike eternal torment, there was purpose in the pain: integration, healing, and rebirth.

Hell became subjective, existential. It was the battlefield of the self. Films like Inception, The Matrix, and What Dreams May Come portrayed hell not as a furnace but a fractured mind. A labyrinth of guilt, illusion, and despair. A punishment shaped by the soul itself. In these modern myths, salvation is no longer divine—it is chosen, wrestled from within.

But even as philosophy softened Hell, institutions sharpened it. In the Middle Ages, Hell became a weapon. A tool of fear, wielded to enforce obedience. It loomed behind pulpits and thrones. Priests and kings used it to frighten dissenters, heretics, and witches into silence.

In the Inquisitions, the flames of Hell found earthly mirrors. Torture chambers became precursors to damnation. Confession was demanded not for truth, but to save the soul. Fear of the afterlife was used to justify horrors in this one. The image of eternal fire was burned into art, sermons, and law. Not as liberation. As control.

Today, in a world growing more secular, many no longer believe in a literal Hell. The fire is myth. The torment, a tool of history. For some, Hell is an outdated relic of control and superstition. But it remains. It persists in language, in symbol, in fear. It lives in trauma, addiction, despair. It clings to cycles of abuse, systems of oppression, places where hope has died. Some now see Hell as a state of being, not a place: A marriage turned cruel. A mind lost to sorrow. A child's hunger in a world of excess. Hell becomes what we fail to heal. And yet—fire transforms. The journey through Hell, as myth teaches us, is not always a condemnation. In stories old and new, those who descend also return: Ishtar, Orpheus, Jesus, Dante, even Lucifer in his way. The underworld is not the end. It is the forge. The darkness is a teacher. The suffering, a mirror.

Hell asks: What have you denied? What must you release? Who are you, when everything else is stripped away?

Whether eternal or imagined, cosmic or psychological, Hell reflects our deepest truths. Our fears of judgment. Our longing for justice. Our hunger for meaning in pain. And perhaps that is Hell's true purpose—not to punish, but to challenge. To ask if we are willing to walk through fire to reclaim ourselves.

6. WORSHIP AND FEAR - THE DUAL NATURE OF DEMONS

They arrive in whispers and fire, in protection and punishment. Feared, invoked, cursed, and adored—demons have always walked a line between horror and holiness. Long before they were cast as tempters of saints or exorcised in sacred rites, demons were spirits of influence, neither wicked nor divine, but something older. Something other.

In ancient Greece, they were called daimōnes—beings of air and spirit. Not monsters, but guides, inspirations, and guardians. Socrates spoke of his daimōn as a voice of conscience. Plato viewed them as intermediary spirits, messengers between mortals and the divine. Like the genius of Rome, the daimōn was not evil—it was the flicker of insight, the tug of fate, the breath of unseen forces moving through the world.

But as theology shifted—from polytheism to monotheism, from complexity to dualism—the spirits that once guided were recast as threats. The Greek daimōn became the Christian demon. This transformation, slow and deliberate, was not just linguistic—it was doctrinal. As Christianity and certain branches of Judaism evolved, they no longer had room for spirits that served neither God nor Satan. The grey had to become black or white. Influenced by Zoroastrian dualism, early monotheists reimagined neutral spirits as agents of corruption, temptation, and rebellion. What had once inspired philosophy now whispered blasphemy. The daimōn became dangerous. Unclean. Evil.

In the ancient Near East, spirits called shedim walked beside humans. Some were chaotic, others protective. They haunted deserts and dreams, but they were also summoned, respected, and even appeased. As with many cultures, the boundaries between gods, demons, and ancestors were fluid. One generation's deity might become the next's warning.

With the rise of monotheism, this fluidity solidified into division. Goddesses like Ishtar, worshipped for centuries, were labeled corrupting forces. Spirits of the wild were branded demonic. Former deities were demonized—not because they had changed, but because the stories had. Their altars fell. Their names became curses.

In early Christianity, thinkers like Theodoret reframed the entire pantheon of Greek gods as demons—immoral tricksters misleading humanity. What had once been Zeus, Apollo, or Pan became malicious spirits, eager to lure souls from the path of salvation.

But demonization did not erase the function of these spirits. People still called upon them—quietly, carefully. Across ancient cultures, demons were tools as much as terrors. In Egypt, priests summoned spirits in healing rituals. In Babylonia, exorcists invoked Lamashtu and Pazuzu, not just to banish them—but to control them. In Greece and Rome, magical papyri included demon names alongside divine invocations. These spirits were dangerous—but they were also powerful. And power, in the hands of those who understood it, could be harnessed. Today, that tension still lives.

In modern demonolatry, spirits like Azazel, Belial, or Lilith are not condemned, but honored. They are seen as guides, mentors, and archetypes of transformation. To some, Azazel represents the bearer of forbidden knowledge—the flame that forges the self. Lilith becomes the voice of sovereignty, the shadow of feminine power long denied. These beings are no longer exiled in fear—they are invoked with reverence.

Here, demons are not evil—they are truths we are taught to fear. Truths about desire, will, freedom, and rebellion.

To worship a demon is not necessarily to kneel before malevolence. Sometimes, it is to listen to the voice others silence. To step outside the boundary stones of orthodoxy and ask: Who benefits when the divine is divided? Who chose which spirits became saints and which became devils?

Throughout history, demons have been both reflections of our shadow and gatekeepers of forgotten wisdom. They frighten us because they remind us of what we've buried. They tempt us because they offer what we've been told to reject. To fear them is natural. To respect them is ancient. To understand them—is power.

The Role of Demons in Folklore and Witchcraft

Demons have long danced on the fringes of folklore and witchcraft—not only as shadows of fear, but as figures of power, knowledge, and pact.

Throughout history, they have served not merely as malevolent forces to flee from, but as spirits to be called, bargained with, and revered. Their roles were not fixed in evil—they were shaped by culture, by fear, and by those who dared to work with them in secret.

In the villages and forests of medieval Europe, where folklore and fear walked hand-in-hand, demons were said to aid witches in acts both wondrous and wicked. They were familiars, protectors, teachers, and sometimes, executioners—depending on who told the tale.

To the Church, these spirits were the agents of Satan, summoned by the damned to corrupt and deceive. But to the people—those who whispered charms by firelight and buried tokens at crossroads—they were tools. Spirits of the old ways, born from a world that did not separate nature from magic, or power from peril.

At the heart of these stories lies one of the most enduring images in the Western imagination: the witch's pact with a demon. In the lore of the witch trials, this pact was more than folklore—it was doctrine. Authorities claimed that witches signed their souls away in dark ceremonies, marking their flesh with symbols of allegiance. These marks—often natural blemishes, scars, or birthmarks—became known as the witch's mark, supposedly left behind by the demon who sealed the bargain. But what did the pact truly mean?

Beneath the accusations of heresy and sin, the demon's pact was a symbol of autonomy. A rejection of divine hierarchy. A spiritual rebellion.

It allowed the practitioner to access power outside the sanctioned paths of church and priesthood—to walk their own road.

In folklore, these pacts granted witches the ability to command spirits, heal or harm, travel invisibly, or gain forbidden knowledge. In reality, they often reflected deeper fears: of women with knowledge, of people outside societal norms, of spiritual agency that defied the Church.

Demonology texts of the early modern period, such as Malleus Maleficarum and Demonolatry by Nicolas Rémy, cataloged demons with obsessive detail—naming their ranks, their signs, and the ways witches might summon them. These works transformed folk spirits into an organized infernal hierarchy, echoing the heavenly choirs they opposed.

Yet beneath the hysteria, a quieter truth remained: for those practicing folk magic, hedgecraft, or herbal healing, demons were not always evil. They were spirits of the wild, ancient and unpredictable, but capable of offering aid—if approached with respect and knowledge.

In grimoires such as The Lesser Key of Solomon, we see remnants of this old approach: demons as intelligences, summoned not through desperation, but ritual, order, and intent. These texts reflect a worldview where working with demons was not always sinful—it was a practice of control, negotiation, and mastery.

The witch, in this context, is not merely a servant of darkness, but a mediator between worlds. One who walks the borderlands between spirit and flesh, between light and shadow. In calling upon spirits, the witch does not surrender—but engages, challenges, harnesses. It is this image that has endured—not just in horror, but in reclamation.

In modern occultism and witchcraft, especially within Left-Hand Path traditions, the demon is once again seen as a teacher. Not of sin, but of sovereignty. Not of damnation, but of spiritual power reclaimed.

The medieval period, particularly during the height of the Church's power in Europe, was marked by a profound fear of demons. This fear was not a vague superstition, but a potent force deeply embedded in the social, religious, and political fabric of the time. Demons were seen as active agents of evil, intricately linked to witches, heretics, and remnants of pagan traditions. The Church's efforts to combat these perceived threats fueled widespread persecution and fundamentally shaped a society steeped in the dread of the demonic.

As Christianity expanded across Europe, it frequently encountered pre-Christian beliefs and local deities. To consolidate religious authority and suppress competing worldviews, the Church rebranded many of these deities as demons. This demonization process was a deliberate strategy to establish monotheism as the only legitimate religious structure, relegating all other spiritual expressions to heresy and devilry. As such, fear of demons became an effective instrument of control, drawing rigid boundaries between sanctioned worship and forbidden practices.

This fear reached its zenith during the witch trials of the late medieval and early modern periods. The Church taught that witches were in league with the devil, using demonic forces to harm society. The infamous Malleus Maleficarum ("The Hammer of Witches"), written in 1486 by Heinrich Kramer and Jacob Sprenger, codified this belief into a manual for identifying, interrogating, and punishing witches. It portrayed witches—primarily women—as servants of Satan who gained supernatural abilities through demonic pacts. But in truth, the vast majority of those accused were innocent.

The gendered nature of this persecution cannot be overstated. Women—especially those who were older, poor, widowed, midwives, healers, or simply outspoken—bore the brunt of the accusations. Many were targeted not for their actions but for existing outside the narrow expectations of their societies.

During the height of the witch hunts between the 15th and 18th centuries, thousands of women across Europe and North America were tried and executed. These trials were fueled by fear, religious fanaticism, and social control. In places like Salem, Massachusetts, women were condemned on flimsy evidence such as dreams, rumors, and spectral testimony. In Scotland, entire communities turned against women they had known their whole lives, resulting in imprisonment, torture, and executions.

These women were not wicked or supernatural—they were scapegoated, silenced, and erased. The idea of the witch became a tool of oppression, used to punish those who resisted conformity or who simply existed on the fringes. Reclaiming the image of the witch today is, for many, an act of resistance and remembrance. It is a way to honor the lives and legacies of those who suffered and to transform the symbol of the witch into one of empowerment, resilience, and spiritual sovereignty.

As R. I. Moore explores in The Formation of a Persecuting Society, the Church's fear of demons was part of a broader strategy to enforce religious orthodoxy. Heresy trials and the Inquisition were not merely about rooting out theological errors but maintaining control over social and cultural life. Demons and their supposed human allies provided a convenient scapegoat for anxiety about change, disorder, and nonconformity.

Heinrich Kramer's Malleus Maleficarum argued that demons were ever-present, able to influence even seemingly innocent behavior. His text became a foundational guide for inquisitors, reinforcing the belief that demons were real, pervasive, and could corrupt anyone. The association between demons and women was central, rooted in the belief that women were inherently more susceptible to sin and spiritual corruption. As Ronald Hutton argues in The Triumph of the Moon, the witch trials reflected deep cultural fears about social order, gender roles, and religious purity—fears that the concept of demons helped crystallize.

Barbara E. Barber's Witchcraft, Sorcery, and the Supernatural further reveals how accusations of witchcraft were often a means to police social boundaries. The demon became a symbol of the "other"—a dark mirror used to justify persecution and exert dominance over those who deviated from social norms.

Despite this dominant narrative, not all folklore portrayed demons as purely evil. In Mediterranean and Slavic cultures, for example, protective spirits with demonic traits were believed to guard homes and fields. These beings, though fierce, were not malevolent—they were guardians invoked to keep evil at bay.

The concept of the jinn in Islamic and Central Asian traditions also illustrates this duality. Made of smokeless fire, jinn could be dangerous or benevolent. While some, like Iblis, rebelled against divine will, others cooperated with humans, offering aid or wisdom. This complexity mirrors that found in demonological traditions across the world.

In witchcraft and esoteric traditions, demons often took on new roles—no longer just agents of temptation, but symbols of power, transformation, and personal sovereignty. Figures like Lilith, Azazel, and Baphomet became icons of rebellion and liberation. Rather than representing sin, they came to symbolize the pursuit of forbidden knowledge, the breaking of taboos, and the reclamation of personal power.

During the witch trials, accusations of demonic involvement were common, with demons blamed for a wide array of supernatural powers attributed to witches. Trial records describe confessions—often extracted under torture—of consorting with demons for cursing, healing, or necromancy. But these narratives also reveal a deeper human desire for empowerment in a world where authority sought to suppress autonomy.

Across the globe, many traditions preserved more balanced views of spirits labeled as "demons." In African and Afro-Caribbean religions like Vodou, powerful spirits (lwa) are neither wholly good nor evil. They demand respect, and in return, they offer guidance, healing, and protection. Similarly, in Indigenous American beliefs, mischievous or trickster spirits challenge humans to grow and confront their limitations.

In Norse mythology, the line between deity and demon is blurred. Figures like Loki, Fenrir, and the Jotnar (giants) are not evil per se, but embody forces of chaos and change. Loki, a trickster god associated with mischief and disruption, plays both helpful and destructive roles in the mythic narrative. His actions bring about Ragnarok, the end of the world—but also the possibility of renewal.

Ultimately, demons in folklore and witchcraft are not static figures. They have evolved alongside human fears, desires, and spiritual quests. Whether feared or revered, they remain symbols of transformation. They challenge societal norms, offer forbidden wisdom, and illuminate the darker paths of spiritual exploration. In this way, demons continue to speak to something primal within the human experience—a hunger for power, mystery, and the untamed forces that dwell just beyond the edges of the known world.

In modern witchcraft, demons continue to play a complex role that reflects both ancient beliefs and contemporary interpretations of spirituality. Unlike in earlier periods, where demons were almost universally feared and associated with evil, the role of demons in modern witchcraft is nuanced, often seen as neither wholly good nor wholly bad. This shift in perception can be attributed to various occult traditions, such as modern Satanism, contemporary Paganism, and modern Demonolatry, which offer new frameworks for interacting with demons.

One prominent view within modern witchcraft, especially in Demonolatry, is that demons are not inherently evil, but rather, complex entities with the potential to provide wisdom, transformation, and empowerment. In works like Modern Demonolatry by S. Connolly and The Devil's Bible by Michael W. Ford, demons are depicted as beings with whom practitioners can form relationships, sometimes seeking their guidance for personal growth and spiritual development. Demonolatry, as a modern spiritual practice, embraces demons not as forces of corruption but as powerful figures to be respected and invoked for empowerment. These practitioners see demons as teachers who help their followers confront the darker aspects of the self—what some might call the "shadow"—and learn to master their own fears, desires, and limitations.

In many modern forms of witchcraft, demons are often understood through a more symbolic lens. Rather than engaging with demons as literal beings, they are sometimes viewed as metaphors for personal struggles, repressed emotions, or aspects of human nature that need to be confronted.

This symbolic interpretation often takes root in the idea that demons are representations of psychological or emotional challenges, and rituals to work with demons are framed as personal empowerment practices.

Ronald Hutton, in Triumph of the Moon, argues that modern Paganism and witchcraft, including their handling of demons, often focus on empowerment and balance rather than on traditional notions of good and evil. In this context, demons are not to be feared or eradicated but integrated as part of the self or the collective unconscious. The depiction of demons as aspects of the psyche is also explored in modern psychological approaches to spirituality, such as those derived from

Jungian psychology, where demons are linked to the repressed or unacknowledged parts of the self.

In contemporary witchcraft, the invocation and work with demons are seen as part of a broader spiritual ecosystem. In addition to personal empowerment, practitioners might seek to use demons in spell work, rituals, or offerings. According to authors like Michael W. Ford in The Devil's Bible, demons can assist in spellcraft, protection, and overcoming obstacles. However, this requires respect and understanding. Unlike the Medieval witch trials, where the mere association with demons was enough to condemn someone, today's practitioners see demons as allies who must be approached with care and intentionality. The relationship between demons and witches today is often one of mutual respect and partnership, albeit with clear boundaries and guidelines for interaction.

by Eliphas Levi

Baphomet

Among the most iconic symbols adopted in modern occultism is Baphomet—a figure that embodies many of the same themes associated with demons in contemporary witchcraft. First popularized in the 19th century by French occultist Eliphas Lévi, Baphomet is often depicted as a winged, goat-headed figure with both male and female attributes, a torch between the horns, and one arm pointing upward and the other downward—a gesture that signifies the Hermetic axiom "As above, so below."

While not a demon in the traditional sense, Baphomet has come to represent balance, transformation, and spiritual liberation. In traditions like Luciferianism and modern Satanism, Baphomet is revered not as a being of evil, but as a symbol of enlightenment, the union of opposites, and the pursuit of hidden knowledge.

The image of Baphomet challenges binary thinking and reflects the broader themes in modern demonology: embracing what is feared, integrating the shadow, and reclaiming power through understanding.

The modern Church of Satan, founded by Anton LaVey in the 1960s, adopted Baphomet as a symbol of its philosophy—representing rebellion, self-worship, and liberation from conventional morality. More recently, The Satanic Temple has used the image of Baphomet to advocate for secularism, religious freedom, and resistance against authoritarianism.

The goat's head, torch, caduceus, and androgynous features in Baphomet's depiction all serve to illustrate deeper esoteric truths: the power of duality, the union of body and spirit, and the path of inner alchemy. Baphomet's torch signifies enlightenment and the search for divine wisdom. The inverted pentagram often associated with Baphomet represents the spirit descending into matter—a symbol of manifestation, not malevolence.

Baphomet's inclusion in modern witchcraft and occultism demonstrates how archetypal power—once feared or misunderstood—can be reclaimed as a source of empowerment and spiritual insight. Just like Lilith or Azazel, Baphomet becomes a mirror through which practitioners can explore their complexity, challenge societal taboos, and deepen their connection to personal truth.

The role of demons in modern witchcraft is fluid and multifaceted, evolving from their medieval and early modern roles as evil entities to more complex and multifactorial representations. In contemporary occult traditions, demons may be seen as spiritual guides, symbols of personal transformation, or rebellious forces against societal constraints.

Whether through practices of Demonolatry, Satanism, or psychological interpretations in modern witchcraft, demons are no longer merely feared but revered in some circles for their power, wisdom, and capacity to foster self-understanding and personal empowerment.

In conclusion, demons in witchcraft today embody a broader spectrum of meanings than ever before, reflecting a modern reinterpretation of these ancient figures as allies, teachers, and transformative forces within spiritual practice.

7. THE CHRISTIANIZATION OF EVIL - RECASTING OLD MYTHS

The spread of Christianity across Europe and the Near East did not merely involve preaching a new faith—it demanded the reimagining of the old. As Christian doctrine took root, it absorbed, reshaped, and ultimately recast the myths and deities of earlier cultures into its own moral framework. What had once been sacred became suspect. Gods became demons. Myths became warnings.

Early Christianity, rooted in a strict monotheistic worldview, viewed all rival powers as threats—be they spiritual, cultural, or political. The old pantheons of gods, with their diverse expressions of fertility, war, love, nature, and death, were incompatible with the idea of a singular, omnipotent deity. And so, these gods were not merely discarded—they were demonized. Their divine attributes were reframed as sinful temptations. Their sacred roles became perversions of Christian morality.

This process was not accidental. It was systematic. The Christian Church, especially from the fourth century onward, sought to establish theological supremacy over the fractured spiritual landscapes it encountered. Pagan gods and spirits, especially those tied to sexuality, nature, and female autonomy, were among the first to be recast as demonic. For example, Pan—the joyful, untamed god of the wild—was gradually reshaped into the image of the devil: goat-legged, horned, grinning.

What once represented vitality and freedom became the icon of depravity and damnation.

Loki, the Norse trickster and god of mischief, was another such figure. Though not evil in his original mythology, Loki embodied chaos and change—forces the Church viewed as antithetical to divine order. He was gradually reinterpreted through a Christian lens as a figure of betrayal and destruction, more in line with Satan than a playful, if dangerous, deity of transformation.

These shifts were not only theological but deeply political. In recasting local deities as demons, the Church undermined existing power structures, aligning itself with rulers and kingdoms seeking to consolidate control. Pagan festivals were repurposed or erased, their gods rewritten as monstrous, dangerous, or seductive. Fertility goddesses became witches. Forest spirits became tempters. The horned gods of the hunt were transformed into the devil himself.

In regions like the British Isles, Gaul, and Scandinavia, where folk traditions ran deep, this demonization was met with resistance. But over generations, the new narratives took hold. Christian monks recorded legends—often with a twist. Sacred groves became haunted woods. The fae became deceivers. Gods became cautionary tales of what happened to those who rebelled against the "true" God.

This redefinition also played a key role in the Church's broader war on magic, divination, and esoteric knowledge. Practices once used to commune with gods, to heal, or to celebrate the cycles of nature, were now labeled heretical. Spirits invoked for guidance were now demons in disguise. Those who practiced the old ways—whether midwives, healers, or seers—were seen as consorting with devils.

As historian Ronald Hutton notes in The Triumph of the Moon, this transformation was part of a larger effort to not only eradicate pagan belief but to rewrite the very cosmology of the world. The Church wasn't content to deny the old gods; it sought to turn them into enemies of salvation.

But despite centuries of suppression, the echoes of these older deities remain. Their forms persist in art, folklore, and the unconscious of the Western world. In some modern spiritualities and occult traditions, these "demons" are being reclaimed—not as evil, but as misunderstood. The horned god, the serpent, the wild woman, the trickster—figures once cast into darkness—are now being seen in a new light.

The Christianization of evil was not the destruction of myth, but its reinvention. And in that reinvention, the boundary between divine and demonic was redrawn—not by the gods themselves, but by those who wrote their names in new languages. It was not the work of individual zealots or isolated missionaries. It was a deliberate, systemic effort by the Church to reshape cultural identities and consolidate both spiritual and temporal authority. By reinterpreting pre-Christian deities as demons, the Church created a stark moral binary—Christianity as light and truth, and everything else as darkness, corruption, and danger.

This transformation was not just theological—it was visual, ritualistic, and embedded into the social fabric through liturgy, law, and art. One of the most striking examples is the image of the horned god. In many pagan traditions, horned deities symbolized fertility, nature, virility, and seasonal cycles. These gods, often wild and ecstatic in form, were revered as expressions of life's primal power. But as Christian imagery developed, these same horns came to symbolize evil.

The devil, especially in late medieval depictions, adopted the features of deities like Pan—goat legs, horns, cloven hooves—an intentional rebranding meant to vilify the old ways. Texts like Malleus Maleficarum (1486), written by Heinrich Kramer, further cemented this connection by explicitly linking pagan rituals to Satanic worship and demonic influence.

This reframing had massive social and cultural consequences. As the Church expanded, it didn't just convert individuals—it reshaped entire worldviews. Communities that once revered healing goddesses, woodland spirits, or agricultural deities were now told these beings were devils in disguise. The belief in demons and evil spirits took center stage, not only in theology but in everyday life. Folk customs were criminalized. Midwives, herbalists, and wise women—once keepers of ancestral knowledge—were accused of sorcery, their practices seen as unholy alliances with infernal forces.

Barbara E. Barber, in Witchcraft, Sorcery, and the Supernatural, explores how this ideological shift fed into the witch hunts and the broader persecution of "heretical" traditions. The Church's denunciation of older belief systems created fertile ground for fear, suspicion, and control. Witchcraft accusations became a tool for regulating society, and demons were the scapegoats used to justify violent suppression of spiritual dissent.

Ronald Hutton, in The Triumph of the Moon, notes that even benign spirits—fairies, land guardians, and household deities—were reimagined through a Christian lens. In rural Europe especially, the Church labeled these beings as demons to discourage lingering folk practices. Nature spirits and local gods became "familiars," helpers to witches in league with the devil.

The divine feminine was particularly targeted: fertility goddesses were demonized as seductresses or child-killers, reinforcing patriarchal dominance and Christian moral codes.

Yet this demonization was not just theological—it was deeply political. By casting pagan deities as demonic, the Church sought to erase the legitimacy of local belief systems and install itself as the sole mediator between humanity and the divine. Heresy became treason. Worship of the old gods became rebellion against heaven. This reframing was essential in maintaining a rigid social hierarchy with the Church at its apex.

The evolution of the devil's image reflects this strategy. The goat legs of Pan, the trident of Poseidon, the tail of Egyptian Set—all were absorbed into the Christian devil's iconography. The message was clear: the gods of old were not just obsolete, they were dangerous.

And yet, total eradication of these traditions proved impossible. Syncretism became a practical tool for conversion. In many cases, the Church repackaged old deities as saints. The Celtic goddess Brigid became Saint Brigid of Kildare. The Roman Saturnalia transformed into Christmas celebrations. Even fertility rites, like those celebrated on May Day, were quietly folded into the Christian calendar. This blending allowed the Church to maintain continuity while redirecting devotion toward Christian figures.

Scandinavia offers a vivid example of this multifaceted transformation. The Christianization of Denmark, Norway, and Sweden was driven largely by royal edict. Kings like Harald Bluetooth and Olaf Tryggvason used force—burning temples, destroying idols, and executing those who resisted. Yet despite these aggressive measures, people continued practicing their ancestral beliefs in secret or in hybridized form. Over time, the Norse gods were not only abandoned but demonized. Loki, once a trickster and a catalyst for change, became associated with chaos, lies, and destruction—a Nordic echo of the Christian Satan.

This transition was never clean. Many communities practiced forms of dual belief for generations, celebrating Christian holidays while honoring the old gods in private. This cultural memory endures, especially in folklore, where pre-Christian motifs subtly survive beneath Christian façades.

The redefinition of festivals was also part of the Church's strategy. Saturnalia became Christmas; Samhain became All Saints' Day and later Halloween. In reframing these sacred times, the Church sought to overwrite the spiritual rhythms of the land, replacing cyclical, nature-based calendars with linear, salvation-based narratives. Ultimately, the Christianization of pagan belief was a layered, strategic, and often violent process. It was about more than salvation—it was about dominance. By transforming old gods into demons and rituals into heresies, the Church established not just a new faith, but an entirely new cosmology—one in which deviation from orthodoxy was cast as rebellion, and the sacred wildness of the old world became something to fear.

And yet, these stories endure. Pan still plays his flute in art and myth. Brigid still brings healing to fires and wells. Loki still whispers in tales of mischief and upheaval. These figures—demonized but not destroyed—remind us that no mythology ever truly dies. It only waits, reshaped and reawakened, in the collective memory of humanity.

8. THE OCCULT AWAKENING - A NEW UNDERSTANDING OF DEMONS

Few figures in religious and occult history embody the paradox of wisdom and control over darkness as powerfully as King Solomon. Revered as a wise and just ruler in biblical texts, Solomon's legacy took on a far more esoteric dimension in later mystical and magical traditions, where he became known not only as a monarch, but as a master magician—one who bent demons to his will through divine wisdom and arcane knowledge.

The Testament of Solomon, a pseudepigraphical work likely composed between the 1st and 5th centuries CE, presents an alternative vision of the biblical king—one steeped in magic and supernatural authority. In this text, Solomon is given a magical ring, engraved with a divine symbol (often imagined as a pentagram or hexagram), allowing him to summon, bind, and command demons. These entities, each possessing unique powers and personalities, are interrogated and tasked with aiding in the construction of the great Temple. Through his command, demons were transformed from chaotic forces into workers of divine architecture.

In this portrayal, Solomon becomes the archetype of the magician-king: not merely a ruler of people, but a sovereign of spirits, wielding divine knowledge to harness the forbidden and turn it toward the light.

This blend of biblical authority and occult mastery would echo through centuries of Western esoteric thought.

Nowhere is Solomon's magical legacy more enduring than in the grimoires of the early modern period, particularly the Lesser Key of Solomon, or Clavicula Salomonis. This text, a cornerstone of ceremonial magic, includes the famed Ars Goetia—a catalog of 72 demons allegedly bound by Solomon himself. Each spirit is described with careful detail: their ranks, appearances, powers, and the sigils needed to summon and command them. These spirits could grant wealth, hidden knowledge, love, or power—if approached with precision and reverence.

The Goetia is not merely a manual of demon summoning—it is a window into a worldview where divine authority and occult practice intersect. The invocation of Solomon's name was not incidental. It anchored the work in sacred legitimacy. The practitioner was not a heretic dabbling in forbidden arts, but a seeker following in the footsteps of a divinely sanctioned figure who had mastered the forces of darkness without being consumed by them.

Solomon's influence extended beyond Christian and magical grimoires into Jewish mysticism and Kabbalistic traditions. In these frameworks, his wisdom is seen as a divine gift—his mastery of demons made possible not by force, but by his profound understanding of the secret names of God and the hidden structure of the cosmos. The Seal of Solomon, his legendary ring, was said to contain not just physical power, but esoteric meaning—sacred geometry, divine names, and the harmonics of creation encoded into its design.

Kabbalistic interpretations of Solomon's demonology often focus not on conquest, but on alignment—of uniting the upper and lower worlds, of harmonizing chaos with order. Within this tradition, controlling demons is not a sinful act, but an act of restoring cosmic balance. The demons, as misunderstood or unruly aspects of creation, are not inherently evil—they are forces to be understood, contained, or redirected toward divine ends.

The Renaissance saw a renewed interest in Solomon's magical reputation. Thinkers like Trithemius and Agrippa invoked his legacy as they redefined the boundaries between religion, science, and magic. For later occultists like Aleister Crowley, Solomon represented the ideal of the magician who moves fluidly between light and shadow, between heaven and the infernal, mastering both without being owned by either.

Solomon's name continued to lend gravitas to magical texts well into the modern era. The *Grand Grimoire*, the *Key of Solomon the King*, and countless other works of ceremonial magic invoke his name and authority to legitimize the summoning of spirits. According to legend, Solomon bound demons and commanded them to labor in building the Temple. In later traditions, particularly in the *Testament of Solomon*, he interrogated these spirits, learned their secrets, and forced them into submission, making him the archetypal exorcist-king.

The Ars Goetia Manuscript

The Ars Goetia stands as one of the most influential and enigmatic grimoires in the history of Western occultism. As the first book within the Lemegeton, or The Lesser Key of Solomon, it focuses on the invocation and command of 72 demons, each meticulously described with their names, sigils, ranks, abilities, and appearances. Compiled in the 17th century, though based on older traditions, the Ars Goetia has become a cornerstone in ceremonial magic, shaping demonological thought for centuries.

At the heart of the Ars Goetia lies the mythic authority of King Solomon—the legendary monarch said to have ruled not only over Israel but over spirits and demons alike. According to legend, Solomon possessed a magical ring, inscribed with a divine seal, granting him dominion over the infernal realm. With this ring and his divine wisdom, he bound the 72 spirits and compelled them to build his temple and reveal the hidden mysteries of creation. These spirits were not merely chaotic forces—they were intelligences of the unseen world, now cataloged and structured into a complex spiritual bureaucracy.

Each demon in the Goetia is presented with remarkable specificity. Bael, the first spirit listed, is said to grant invisibility. Paimon, a mighty king under Lucifer's command, offers knowledge, eloquence, and mastery over arts and sciences. Asmodeus, long known from biblical and apocryphal sources such as the Book of Tobit, appears here as a demon of sensuality, gambling, and desire—no longer a vague figure of lust, but a royal entity with defined powers and attributes.

The rituals described for summoning these spirits are elaborate, rooted in ceremonial magic and requiring precise symbols, incantations, and protective circles. Practitioners are instructed to work within strict parameters—using consecrated tools, invoking divine names, and observing moral discipline—to ensure control and avoid spiritual danger. These instructions echo the notion, seen since the days of Solomon, that commanding demons requires not only arcane knowledge but moral authority and divine sanction.

But the Ars Goetia is more than a manual for summoning. It is a philosophical text wrapped in occult garb—a reflection of the belief that knowledge, even forbidden knowledge, can be a path to transformation. Many modern practitioners do not see the spirits of the Goetia as evil, but as mirrors of the human psyche, offering challenges and insight into one's desires, limitations, and potential. To engage with these spirits is, in a sense, to confront the shadow—the untamed, unconscious self—and draw from it power.

The Goetia has had a profound and lasting impact on Western esotericism. Influential occultists like Eliphas Lévi, S. L. MacGregor Mathers, and Aleister Crowley drew heavily from its structure and symbolism. Crowley's own version of the Ars Goetia, published with annotations and ritual modifications, further popularized the text within Thelemic and modern magical circles. For them, the demons were not simply infernal agents but gateways to power, knowledge, and spiritual awakening—provided the magician was strong enough to wield such forces.

Its influence, however, is not confined to grimoires and ritual circles. The demons of the Goetia have leapt into the collective imagination through literature, film, music, and games. In these modern incarnations, they are often portrayed as complex figures—regal, cunning, even tragic—echoing the ambiguity that has always surrounded their mythos.

The Renaissance and the Rebirth of the Demonic Mind

The Renaissance, spanning the 14th to 17th centuries, was not only a cultural rebirth of classical art, literature, and science—it was also a spiritual awakening. Beneath the gilded surface of paintings and philosophical discourse stirred a deeper current: an occult revival that sought to reclaim humanity's connection to the cosmos through ancient wisdom, magical practice, and esoteric thought. This period did not merely tolerate mystery—it revered it, and within that reverence, demons, gods, and angels were reimagined as forces to be studied, summoned, and understood.

Much of this revival can be traced to the rediscovery and translation of ancient manuscripts—many of which flowed into Western Europe after the fall of Constantinople in 1453. Byzantine scholars brought with them lost texts of Hermeticism, Neoplatonism, alchemy, and Jewish mysticism. These became the seeds of Renaissance occultism, flourishing in the intellectual gardens of Florence, Rome, and beyond.

Among the most influential were the Corpus Hermeticum, a series of mystical dialogues attributed to Hermes Trismegistus. Translated into Latin by Marsilio Ficino in the 15th century, these texts proclaimed that humanity contained a divine spark and could, through knowledge and spiritual refinement, rise to commune with the divine.

Ficino, a Neoplatonist and astrologer, helped frame occult study as not demonic, but divine. His belief in "natural magic"—magic derived from celestial influences—taught that understanding planetary energies and harmonizing with them could elevate the soul, restore health, and bring spiritual illumination.

Christian Kabbalah soon joined this revival. Scholars like Giovanni Pico della Mirandola sought to merge Kabbalistic teachings with Christian theology, believing these ancient mysteries concealed universal truths. In his Oration on the Dignity of Man, Pico declared that humans were uniquely capable of shaping their own spiritual destinies, bridging heaven and earth through philosophy, magic, and divine contemplation.

Alchemy, long misunderstood as a mere quest for gold, was reinterpreted during this period as a symbolic system of transformation—both material and metaphysical. Figures like Paracelsus revolutionized medicine by fusing alchemical philosophy with empirical practice, insisting that illness had spiritual roots and that healing required a balance of elemental and spiritual forces. The alchemist's laboratory became a temple, and the Philosopher's Stone a metaphor for inner perfection.

Astrology, too, thrived during this era. Scholars such as Johannes Kepler navigated the boundary between astronomy and divination, convinced that celestial bodies moved not just in physical orbits, but in accordance with divine will. Astrology was seen as sacred geometry—a cosmic map mirroring the soul's journey on earth.

Magic during the Renaissance was multifaceted and carefully categorized. "Natural magic" sought to manipulate the hidden properties of plants, stones, and stars. "Celestial magic" worked through planetary harmonies and angelic influence. "Demonic magic," the most feared and misunderstood, involved summoning spirits not through divine grace but through compulsion and pact.

While condemned by the Church, this last category drew the interest of occult philosophers eager to understand the full spectrum of spiritual power.

Cornelius Agrippa's Three Books of Occult Philosophy (1533) became the magnum opus of Renaissance magic. Synthesizing astrology, Kabbalah, angelology, and ritual magic, Agrippa argued that true magic was the highest form of philosophy—a divine science through which the soul could ascend toward God. Though deeply pious in tone, his work attracted suspicion. The line between sacred knowledge and heresy was perilously thin, and many who studied these texts walked it knowingly.

This era also reimagined spiritual beings through a philosophical and symbolic lens. Pagan deities, once literal objects of worship, were increasingly seen as archetypes—manifestations of divine principles. Venus represented divine love; Mercury, wisdom and communication; Mars, the will to action. Similarly, demons were no longer regarded solely as agents of sin but as spiritual intelligences—some hostile, some neutral, others even enlightening—whose natures reflected deeper cosmic forces.

John Dee, the famed English mathematician, astrologer, and alchemist, exemplified this approach. With his scryer Edward Kelley, he sought communion with angelic beings, recording vast "angelic" communications in a language known as Enochian. Dee's Monas Hieroglyphica symbolized his vision: that all of creation, both visible and invisible, could be deciphered and understood through sacred geometry and divine correspondence.

Within this intellectual ferment, grimoires such as The Key of Solomon, Heptameron, Arbatel of Magic, and the Goetia circulated among scholars and magicians, often in secret.

These Latin texts were filled with invocations to spirits once feared and now reconsidered. Demons were no longer seen simply as tempters or agents of chaos, but as complex beings offering forbidden wisdom, challenges to be overcome, and gateways to spiritual evolution.

The magician no longer fled from the demonic but sought to engage with it—armed with sigils, names of power, and the understanding that to know the self, one must also navigate the darkness. Renaissance thinkers sought not to destroy or deny pre-Christian mythologies but to reinterpret them—casting old gods as symbols, demons as masks of shadowed knowledge, and angels as intermediaries of divine light. The occult sciences of this era laid a foundation for what would later become psychology, metaphysics, and even modern spiritual movements.

The Renaissance did not banish the demons—it gave them new names, forms, and purpose, setting the stage for their continued evolution in the hidden chambers of the Western mystery tradition.

The Enlightenment – Rationality and the Reinterpretation of Demons

As the Renaissance gave way to the Enlightenment, the cultural landscape of Europe shifted dramatically. From the late 17th to early 19th centuries, the Age of Reason emerged as a defining movement—championing rationality, empirical inquiry, and the scientific method. With this intellectual revolution came a growing skepticism toward mysticism, magic, and the occult traditions that had flourished just a century before.

Where the Renaissance had embraced the divine mysteries of Hermeticism, alchemy, astrology, and angelic hierarchies, the Enlightenment sought clarity, categorization, and control. Thinkers like Voltaire, Denis Diderot, and David Hume dismissed occult sciences as relics of ignorance. Astrology, once consulted by kings and scholars, fell from favor as the celestial mechanics of Newton replaced the mystical alignments of the stars. Alchemy, long a spiritual and philosophical pursuit, was stripped of its esoteric symbolism and reborn as modern chemistry in the hands of scientists like Robert Boyle and Antoine Lavoisier.

In this climate of growing secularism, demons were no longer seen as literal agents of temptation or servants of hell, but increasingly reframed as symbols—remnants of a mythic worldview now under rational scrutiny. Yet even as the Enlightenment cast aside superstition, it could not wholly banish the supernatural. Interest in the occult persisted, reshaped by psychology, metaphysics, and the hunger for meaning beyond cold empiricism.

A striking example of this new interpretation is found in the writings of Emanuel Swedenborg (1688–1772), a mystic and scientist who envisioned the spiritual world as intricately linked to the moral and emotional states of the soul. In his visionary theology, angels and demons were not external enemies or allies but reflections of internal conditions. Demons represented human vices—greed, pride, selfishness—while angels symbolized the soul's capacity for love, wisdom, and divine order. Swedenborg's vision offered a psychological and metaphysical approach to spiritual forces, bridging Enlightenment rationalism with mystical insight.

Toward the end of the Enlightenment, the Romantic movement began to reclaim the imagination, emotion, and mystery that reason had tried to eclipse. Romantics such as Goethe, Blake, and Shelley found inspiration in the very occult traditions Enlightenment thinkers had dismissed. They saw in myth and magic not superstition, but symbolism—deep truths cloaked in allegory, encoded in the language of gods and demons. The demon became less a threat to the soul and more a mirror of the inner self: chaotic, creative, dangerous, and sublime.

This changing perspective laid the groundwork for the occult revival of the 19th century, when spiritualism, Theosophy, and ceremonial magic would reawaken the Western fascination with demons, not as agents of evil, but as emissaries of transformation.

Figures like Aleister Crowley epitomized this new understanding. Founder of Thelema, Crowley embraced the demon not as a tempter, but as a symbol of liberation and self-sovereignty. His teachings called for the integration of all aspects of the self—light and dark, divine and bestial. In The Book of the Law, he proclaimed, "Do what thou wilt shall be the whole of the Law," elevating personal will above social and religious constraints.

For Crowley and his followers, demons were not to be feared, but summoned—engaged with as guides, challengers, and gatekeepers to hidden knowledge.

This reinterpretation was echoed in modern demonology, where demons are approached with reverence, not hostility. They become symbols of self-mastery, transformation, and spiritual autonomy—each embodying a different aspect of human potential.

No longer relegated to the shadows of hell, demons entered the world of modern psychology. Influenced by thinkers like Carl Jung, occultists began to view demons as archetypes of the unconscious—personifications of the "shadow self," those repressed aspects of the psyche that must be acknowledged and integrated for wholeness to occur. In this light, demonic figures were not evil per se, but necessary elements of personal alchemy.

As this shift gained momentum, popular culture followed suit. Literature, film, music, and art began to depict demons not as mindless monsters but as tragic, seductive, or even sympathetic beings. In Neil Gaiman's American Gods, demons walk among mortals, struggling with fading relevance and divine identity. In shows like Supernatural or Lucifer, demons wrestle with moral complexity, free will, and redemption. They became antiheroes—symbols of rebellion, temptation, and the human desire to break boundaries.

The 21st century has continued this trajectory. In occult circles, demons are increasingly viewed as guides on the path of self-knowledge. Practices such as demonolatry embrace these entities as spiritual partners, each one offering unique lessons or powers to those who seek them with respect and intention.

The figure once feared as a corrupter of souls is now seen, in some traditions, as a revealer of truth, a teacher of forbidden wisdom.

The Enlightenment may have attempted to cast out demons in the name of reason—but instead, it transformed them. Stripped of their medieval horror and reborn through Romantic, psychological, and esoteric frameworks, demons became vessels of personal transformation, symbols of both danger and potential. Whether seen as spirits, archetypes, or metaphors, their enduring presence reflects humanity's unending desire to confront the unknown—both within and beyond the self.

9. A World Divided
– Control vs. Reverence

In the long and evolving tale of demonology, two distinct paths emerge: the commanding rituals of Solomonic magic and the reverent philosophy of demonolatry. Though both engage with demonic forces, they do so from fundamentally different worldviews. One seeks dominion—tools to be wielded. The other seeks communion—wisdom to be honored. At their core lies a profound question: are demons to be conquered, or are they to be understood?

At the heart of Solomonic tradition lies the legendary figure of King Solomon, said to possess not only extraordinary wisdom but dominion over spirits and demons alike. In grimoires such as The Lesser Key of Solomon and The Testament of Solomon, the magician is portrayed as a master of divine authority—armed with sacred symbols, empowered by the names of God, and capable of binding demons to his will. Through the Seal of Solomon, ritual circles, and invocations, demons are commanded, constrained, and compelled into service.

This practice is rooted in the belief that demons are rebellious entities— fallen beings from a divine order—whose power is dangerous and must be tightly controlled. Solomonic magic treats the spiritual world as a hierarchy, with the practitioner positioned above the demon by virtue of divine mandate. The demon is a servant, a force to be subdued, often through threats, divine names, or celestial authority. Whether the magician seeks knowledge, wealth, or protection, the ultimate goal is control—to bend the will of the demonic to human ends.

This framework is shaped by the theological lens of its time—especially the Christian worldview that casts demons as the antithesis of divine order. In this cosmology, summoning a demon is not a partnership but a confrontation, a test of dominance that hinges on purity, preparation, and precise ritual.

In sharp contrast, demonolatry emerges as a path of honor and reverence. Rather than commanding demons, practitioners of demonolatry seek to form relationships with them—not through domination, but through devotion, respect, and spiritual kinship. Far from seeing demons as adversaries, demonolators approach them as ancient intelligences, spiritual guides, and even divine beings in their own right.

Here, demons are not judged by a moral binary of good and evil. Instead, they are seen as archetypal forces of transformation—agents of change, guardians of hidden knowledge, and embodiments of the shadow self.

The rituals of demonolatry are devotional rather than coercive, involving offerings, meditations, prayers, and sigils designed to open communication and foster mutual growth. The practitioner does not seek to bind, but to understand—and in doing so, to evolve.

Demonolatry often draws on Luciferian and Left-Hand Path philosophies, embracing personal autonomy, rebellion against dogma, and the exploration of the self's darker aspects. It is a practice of empowerment—not through subjugating the other, but through embracing the other within. In this worldview, demons are not obstacles to spiritual growth; they are its catalysts.

The core divergence between Solomonic magic and demonolatry lies not in the demons themselves, but in the magician's approach. In Solomonic tradition, the demon is a tool—subordinate, constrained, used. In demonolatry, the demon is a partner—honored, approached, revered. One path walks with a rod of iron and sacred name, the other with open palms and deliberate humility.

Both traditions, however, reflect humanity's evolving relationship with the unknown. Solomonic magic emerged from a world where control over the spiritual offered a semblance of safety in an uncertain universe. Demonolatry, by contrast, belongs to a modern—and often post-religious—world that seeks meaning in personal sovereignty, internal transformation, and the breaking of inherited chains.

Where one sees danger, the other sees potential. Where one builds barriers, the other builds bridges. Through this dichotomy, we glimpse the deeper truth: the demonic has always served as a mirror—reflecting not only the forces we fear, but the ones we long to understand. Whether through command or communion, control or reverence, the human interaction with demons remains one of mystery, risk, and revelation. And perhaps, in this contrast, we see not just two magical traditions—but two expressions of what it means to be human: to wrestle with the unknown, to reach beyond our limits, and to decide whether we face the darkness with a sword—or an outstretched hand.

While both Solomonic magic and demonolatry have deeply shaped the Western occult tradition, I personally find the model of reverence and relationship offered by demonolatry far more aligned with my own path. The idea of commanding or subjugating spiritual beings feels at odds with the mutual respect that I believe should define all spiritual practice. Still, the historical significance of Solomonic traditions cannot be overstated.

This divergence in approach—command versus communion, control versus reverence—illustrates the broader philosophical divide that continues to shape modern practices and interpretations. For those drawn to the path of working with demons, it's essential to understand not only the historical context but also the contemporary frameworks that have emerged from these traditions.

Chief among them are the distinct disciplines of *demonolatry* and *demonology*, each offering a different lens through which to view and engage with the demonic. Though they share a common subject, their purposes and methodologies are profoundly different.

Demonolatry or Demonology

Though both concern themselves with the study and interaction with demons, *demonolatry* and *demonology* diverge significantly in perspective, purpose, and practice.

Demonolatry is a spiritual or religious path centered on the veneration or honoring of demons. Rather than viewing them as evil or malevolent, practitioners see demons as powerful, divine, or enlightening beings. Within this tradition, demons are not feared but respected—as mentors, guides, or forces of transformation. Rituals in demonolatry may include offerings, prayers, or invocations designed to deepen one's connection with a specific entity. These practices are often highly personal, grounded in mutual respect rather than domination. The focus is not on control, but on communion—a relationship that fosters spiritual insight, self-discovery, and empowerment.

Demonology, by contrast, is the academic or theological study of demons. It is more analytical than devotional. A demonologist may explore the origins, functions, and cultural representations of demons across history—from the ancient Near East and Greco-Roman traditions to medieval Christian theology and beyond. This field examines how demons have functioned within religious systems, myths, literature, folklore, and psychological frameworks. While some demonologists may engage in spiritual or magical practices, the primary focus is usually knowledge: to understand, categorize, and interpret rather than to worship or form spiritual relationships.

The difference is, at its core, one of intent. Demonolatry seeks engagement; demonology seeks understanding. The former views demons as beings with whom one may form bonds of reverence and trust, while the latter often regards demons through a more detached lens—sometimes as symbolic of humanity's fears and moral boundaries, sometimes as literal agents of disorder.

In summary: Demonolatry is a path of reverence and spiritual interaction. Demonology is a study of concept and cultural legacy. Both are rooted in a fascination with the demonic, but they travel very different roads—one inward and devotional, the other outward and analytical.

10. Demons in the Modern Age— The Changing Narrative

As we've explored throughout this book, the image of the demon has evolved dramatically over time. From divine adversaries and cosmic rebels to spiritual guides and psychological archetypes, demons have shifted from the realm of strict religious dogma into a more symbolic, personal, and culturally fluid space. This transformation reflects broader shifts in society—secularism, the rise of psychology, the influence of pop culture, and the resurgence of alternative spiritualities.

Contemporary psychology often views demons as metaphors for internal struggles. Freud's theories of the unconscious and repression, along with Carl Jung's concept of the shadow self, helped recast demons as aspects of our own psyche—those hidden or rejected parts of ourselves that must be acknowledged and integrated. In this light, demons are no longer purely external threats, but inner forces demanding recognition: symbols of addiction, depression, anxiety, grief, or rage. Confronting these inner demons becomes an act of healing, growth, and personal evolution.

In popular culture, demons have become increasingly complex. Horror films like The Exorcist (1973), Rosemary's Baby (1968), and Hereditary (2018) still evoke primal fear, but they also explore deeper psychological and existential themes—trauma, guilt, spiritual disillusionment.

In many stories, demons are no longer one-dimensional villains but beings with agency, sometimes even sympathy. These portrayals reflect a modern fascination with moral ambiguity and the darker corners of the human experience.

Modern occultism has also reimagined demons. In works by authors like Michael W. Ford and S. Connolly, demons are no longer viewed solely as malevolent forces but as allies in personal transformation. Practices such as demonolatry emphasize mutual respect, spiritual autonomy, and the pursuit of hidden knowledge. As new age and esoteric traditions continue to blur the line between religion and personal spiritual practice, the definition of "demon" expands—no longer confined to the dichotomy of good versus evil, but existing within a larger, more nuanced spiritual landscape.

Today, demons continue to fascinate, disturb, and inspire. They appear in everything from high fantasy and tabletop role-playing games to viral horror stories and modern spirituality. What once symbolized pure evil now serves as a mirror—reflecting our fears, desires, unresolved pain, and unclaimed power. They provoke us not only to question what we believe, but to explore why we fear, and what that fear may conceal.

The demon has survived exorcisms, inquisitions, and centuries of religious condemnation. Now it lives on in new forms—as metaphor, muse, scapegoat, and guide. But in the midst of all this transformation, one period of modern history stands out as a particularly volatile clash between fear and fascination.

Before we can fully understand the present-day spiritual and cultural landscape of demons, we must revisit a time not so long ago—when fear of the demonic exploded into mass hysteria, devastating lives and leaving a lasting mark on public consciousness.

Enter the Satanic Panic. A moral hysteria that swept across the United States in the 1980s and early 1990s. Driven by media sensationalism, religious anxiety, and cultural unease, it cast a wide net of suspicion over everything from heavy metal music to Dungeons & Dragons. At the center of the panic were alarming but largely unfounded claims of Satanic ritual abuse (SRA), in which secret cults were alleged to be abusing and murdering children in the name of Satan.

The panic was ignited in part by the 1980 book *Michelle Remembers*, in which psychiatrist Lawrence Pazder and his patient Michelle Smith claimed to uncover repressed memories of childhood abuse by a Satanic cult. Though lacking corroborating evidence, the book was presented as fact and quickly captured the public imagination. The media, eager for scandal, amplified similar allegations. In 1983, the McMartin Preschool trial—a case involving supposed ritual abuse in California—became one of the most expensive and publicized trials in U.S. history, despite ultimately resulting in no convictions.

Television specials, particularly Geraldo Rivera's 1988 program *Devil Worship: Exposing Satan's Underground*, lent further credibility to the panic. Rivera's documentary presented sensational claims of widespread Satanic cult activity, reinforcing public fears without substantiating evidence. Talk shows like *Oprah* and *Sally Jessy Raphael* featured alleged ex-Satanists and reformed occultists, often with dubious backgrounds, who claimed firsthand knowledge of ritual abuse and Satanic conspiracies.

Therapists and law enforcement officials, influenced by these narratives, began identifying supposed SRA cases using controversial methods like recovered memory therapy, hypnosis, and suggestive questioning.

These techniques often led to the creation of false memories, resulting in wrongful accusations, prosecutions, and long-term damage to innocent individuals and families.

The consequences were devastating. Innocent people were imprisoned, children were traumatized by coercive questioning, and public trust in social institutions eroded. Subcultures such as goth, punk, and heavy metal were vilified, with bands like Judas Priest and Slayer accused of promoting Satanism. Games like Dungeons & Dragons were linked to occultism and blamed for encouraging delusion or suicide. Even ordinary interests in magic, tarot, or horror films became cause for suspicion.

At its core, the Satanic Panic reflected deep societal fears—about changing family dynamics, shifting gender roles, growing secularism, and the erosion of traditional religious authority. The demon became a scapegoat for moral anxieties, and those who explored alternative spiritualities or unconventional lifestyles were often painted with the same brush.

The legacy of the Satanic Panic continues to shape public perception of demons and the occult. It reinforced the idea that all demonic entities were agents of evil, erasing their nuanced mythological and spiritual origins. Demons were portrayed exclusively through a Christian lens—as tempters, corrupters, or possessors—rather than as complex figures with varied roles in different cultures. Practices like witchcraft, ceremonial magic, and even yoga or meditation were, at times, implicated in imaginary networks of Satanic influence.

Hollywood contributed to this demonization. Films like *The Conjuring* and *The Exorcism of Emily Rose* present demons as malevolent entities whose only purpose is to terrorize and destroy. These portrayals, while often compelling, continue to frame demons as purely evil, reinforcing the fear-based narratives born of the Satanic Panic. Ancient deities like Baal or

Azazel are reduced to grotesque villains, stripped of their rich mythological context. Yet, alongside these distortions, there has also been a cultural pushback. In recent years, modern practitioners, scholars, and spiritual seekers have begun to reclaim demonized figures. Books, podcasts, and media platforms now challenge simplistic portrayals of demons, offering alternative perspectives rooted in history, mythology, and personal experience. Figures like Lilith, Baphomet, and Azazel are being reexamined, not as symbols of evil, but as archetypes of power, resistance, or shadow integration.

The Satanic Panic, in retrospect, reveals more about society's fear of the unknown than about demons themselves. It teaches us how quickly misinformation and cultural anxiety can distort our understanding of spiritual figures—and how necessary it is to approach such topics with nuance, critical thinking, and an openness to diverse traditions. This book seeks to be part of that broader reclamation—an invitation to reconsider what demons are, what they represent, and what they can teach us.

11. The Forgotten Gods

Now you've followed the history of demons, from the ancient world to modern times. Before we begin exploring the practical side of working with demons, we'll take a dive into the old grimoires — the texts that have shaped how these beings are summoned, understood, and worked with — and uncover what they can still teach us today.

As we have explored through out these pages, many any of the entities listed in grimoires, invoked or forced to submission through ritual were once deities, spirits, or guardians in pre-Christian traditions—revered, respected, and often deeply embedded in the cycles of life, death, and nature. Over time, through the processes of Christianization, colonization, and social control, these figures were reframed as dangerous, evil, or corrupt. To understand demons even further, we can study their history and the grimoires written about them.

Among countless infernal names, King Belial emerges with a past woven in fascination and vivid legend. Before names had weight and before good and evil were divided by priest or prophet, there was a whisper among men—a word, not a name. *Beli-ya'al*, they called it in the ancient tongue. It meant "without worth." No master, no yoke. It clung to those who defied the sacred order, men who laughed at laws, who thrived in chaos. Sons of Belial, they said. Not yet a figure, but a force. A shadow in the hearts of the lawless. But time is a fire that sharpens legends.

Long before Belial appeared as a demon in Christian grimoires or occult texts, he was feared and named in the writings of an isolated sect living in the desert: the Essenes. These men and women, driven by a fierce devotion to purity and righteousness, saw the world divided between light and darkness — between those loyal to God and those corrupted by evil. In their sacred texts, now known as the Dead Sea Scrolls, Belial is no minor tempter or mischievous spirit. He is the Prince of Darkness, the leader of all forces opposed to God. His very name — sometimes translated as "worthless" or "without value" — marked him as the embodiment of chaos, lawlessness, and ruin. The Essenes believed that Belial controlled legions of spirits and human agents, working tirelessly to lead people into sin, to corrupt the Temple, and to wage war against the *Sons of Light* — the true, faithful followers.

The *War Scroll* paints a vivid, almost cinematic picture of this coming confrontation: a great apocalyptic battle where Belial's army of the wicked will rise against the righteous, only to be defeated by divine intervention. For the Essenes, Belial was not just a myth; he was an ever-present threat, a force behind political corruption, spiritual decay, and moral collapse.

What harmony is there between Christ and Belial? asked Paul, though the answer was already clear: none. In Paul's words, Belial was not just a figure — he was the embodiment of lawlessness, corruption, and the forces that stand in opposition to the divine. At this point in history, Belial was less a demon with horns and a throne, and more a symbol: the spirit of rebellion, of worthlessness, pagans, and the forces that stand in opposition to the divine.

But over time, Belial's image became more than just a warning against sin. He began to emerge as a symbol — for those cast aside by rigid systems of control, for the rebellious, the unwanted, the untamed. What once described a condition — *běli-yaʻal*, the worthless or the rejected — hardened into a name, and then into a presence. As the centuries passed, Belial stepped out of the shadows of metaphor and into the vivid landscape of demonology, taking his place among the great infernal kings.

To speak his name was no longer just to speak of wickedness, but to invoke the memory of a being who stood, defiantly, at the margins — the lord of those whom the righteous had left behind.

And so Belial's name passed through generations. No longer the spirit of worthlessness, but its crowned king. In the dim candlelight he was invoked—sometimes worshipped, more often feared.

They wrote of him in forbidden books: the Goetia, the Pseudomonarchia Daemonum, the Dictionnaire Infernal. Always the same: a king without chains, beautiful and treacherous. His eyes saw through lies because he was made of them. He arrived in a chariot of fire, pulled by beasts, offering power to the desperate and ruin to the careless. Eighty legions marched behind him, but he walked alone. Even Hell could not claim him fully.

Magicians warned: he will lie unless bound. He grants titles, secrets, and thrones—but always at a price. A life. A soul. A truth. He cannot be summoned without sacrifice, for he answers to no master, not even the Devil himself. Some whispered he was the second to fall after Lucifer, and the most dangerous because he fell not from pride, but from defiance.

In alchemical circles, Belial was the dross—the false gold, the corrupted base matter the alchemist must purify. He was the temptation to stop the work halfway, to settle for illusion. Yet in that same corruption lay truth—the truth of self-rule, of standing alone in a world that demands obedience. Some modern magi call him "the spirit of independence." Others fear him as the anchor to the material, the weight that drags the soul from ascension.

In the dark paths of the Qliphoth, he is the gatekeeper to the *Sitra Achra*—the Other Side. There, he no longer tempts with simple sins, but with sovereignty. He does not demand worship, only acknowledgment. Not a demon to kneel before, but a force to meet eye to eye, if you dare.

Belial does not come when called. He comes when challenged. And when he speaks, it is with the voice of those who refused to bow.

Understanding this vision of Belial is crucial. It reminds us that the figure we later encounter in medieval demonology has deep roots in ancient apocalyptic thought — a symbol of ultimate opposition, not just a spirit to summon or command.

In the Ars Goetia Belial is one of the most powerful and enigmatic spirits;

> *"The Sixty-eighth Spirit is Belial. He is a mighty and powerful King, created next after Lucifer..."*

Belial is not just summoned—he is enthroned. He does not crawl or claw his way from Hell; he arrives with grace, fire, and majesty, appearing in the form of two beautiful angels seated in a chariot of flame. He is radiant, commanding, terrible in elegance. No grotesque monster or slavering beast—Belial's danger lies in how easily one could trust him.

He speaks sweetly. Offers rise in rank. Wealth, titles, allies and favors from powerful spirits. His promises are irresistible to those hungry for success or revenge. But his gifts are not free.

> *"He distributeth Preferments of Senatorships, and causeth favours of Friends and of Foes. He giveth excellent Familiars..."*

The magician must not treat Belial like a lesser demon. If summoned improperly or without sacrifice, he is known to deceive—"he is not to be trusted without a sacrifice, for he is a great liar."

> *"He must have offerings or sacrifices made unto him, or he will not give true answers unto demands. But then he tarrieth not one hour in the truth, unless he be constrained by Divine Power."*

This is one of the most chilling warnings in the Goetia. Even when he speaks truth, that truth is conditional. Timed and measured. He remains loyal to no one, answering only to those who prove themselves stronger or wiser than he is.

Tools for Summoning according to this text: A magic circle and proper conjuration prayers are essential. The summoner must invoke divine authority—not just magical command, but spiritual superiority—to compel Belial to obey. Sacrifices (in historical context, likely incense or offerings) are often required.

As modern witches and demonolaters, approaching the old grimoires requires more than blind acceptance or rigid reenactment. These texts were written in specific cultural, religious, and historical contexts — shaped by the fears, desires, and limitations of their time. To read them word for word as if they are flawless manuals would be to misunderstand their deeper value. What we can take from the grimoires is symbolism. Each seal, each invocation, each strange instruction is a reflection of a relationship between humans and the unseen. The demons depicted are not just static entities with fixed personalities, but living symbols of desire, fear, knowledge, and transformation.

When we engage with these texts today, we are not bound to mimic their every command; rather, we are invited to interpret them, to draw meaning from their layered language, and to connect their symbols to our own spiritual landscapes. The grimoires can teach us about the power of intention, the art of focus, and the ways humans have always sought to name and navigate the forces that shape their lives.

To work with demons now is not to submit to dusty instructions but to enter into a living dialogue — one shaped by history, yes, but also by personal experience, intuition, and respect. The grimoires are a starting point, not a manual.

Understanding the original context of these beings allows practitioners to approach them with greater depth. We move beyond seeing demons as villains of religious lore and begin to understand them as complex, storied figures—sometimes fallen gods, sometimes protectors, always more than the labels imposed upon them.

Even the hierarchies used in grimoires like the Ars Goetia—where demons are titled kings, dukes, princes, and so on—reflect an attempt to impose order on a spiritual world that was once fluid, relational, and reciprocal. These rankings do not always reflect the ancient status or cultural significance of these entities. Instead, they often mirror feudal systems and Christian worldviews that sought to organize the supernatural into manageable categories, which we will explore further down the line.

The Grimoires

As mentioned earlier in this book, The Ars Goetia is one of the sections in the Lesser Key of Solomon (also known as the Clavicula Salomonis Regis), a famous grimoire (book of magic) attributed to King Solomon. The Ars Goetia specifically deals with the summoning and commanding of 72 demons, providing instructions on how to invoke and control them. It is one of the most well-known parts of the Key of Solomon, and it has been influential in Western occultism, especially in practices involving ritual magic.

The Ars Goetia describes the demons and their abilities, often presenting them as powerful spirits with specific skills or knowledge, such as the ability to grant wisdom, wealth, or power. Each demon is associated with a specific rank or title, and the text provides detailed instructions for rituals, sigils, and other tools necessary for their summoning. These demons are often portrayed as fallen angels, aligning with Christian ideas of demonic beings, though their origins and mythologies vary. In the Ars Goetia, the demons are also categorized by their function and nature, with some being categorized as "great kings," "presidents," or "dukes." Some of the most famous demons include Bael, Paimon, Asmodeus, and Baphomet (the latter, however, appears in later sources). The Ars Goetia has played a key role in the development of Western ceremonial magic and has influenced various occult traditions, including modern demonology, the practices of witchcraft, and even popular culture.

In addition to the Ars Goetia, several other grimoires explore the world of demons and their hierarchies, offering detailed instructions on how to summon, control, or interact with these entities. The Lesser Key of Solomon is divided into different sections, including the Ars Theurgia-

Goetia, which details additional demons, and the Ars Paulina, which addresses angelic forces, but the Goetia remains the most well-known part for dealing with demonic entities.

The Grand Grimoire (also known as The Red Dragon) is one of the most famous of the "Black Grimoires," this book focuses on demonology and magic. It is said to offer instructions on how to summon the devil, as well as various demonic entities. It provides information on their nature, appearances, and how to bind them. The Grand Grimoire emphasizes the idea of pacts with demons and the devil, claiming to provide the secrets of attaining wealth and power.

A comprehensive grimoire of astrological magic, the Picatrix originates from Arabic sources and became influential in Europe during the Renaissance. It provides magical instructions for summoning and working with planetary and demonic forces, though its primary focus is on astrology and cosmology. Some of the demons and spirits described in Picatrix are tied to the celestial spheres and are invoked for magical workings that involve both astrology and alchemy.

The Grimoire of Pope Honorius. This grimoire, often attributed to Pope Honorius III, is a medieval text that provides instructions for summoning demons and conducting rituals, with a particular emphasis on gaining control over spirits. The book includes prayers, rituals, and seals that are used to bind and control demons. It is especially famous for its supposed connection to exorcisms and its claim to grant authority over demons.

The Book of Abramelin is a mystical grimoire dating from the 14th or 15th century, The Book of Abramelin is centered on the process of contacting and summoning one's "Holy Guardian Angel." However, it also discusses the banishment of demons and the establishment of a relationship between the practitioner and both angels and demons. The book is structured around a six-month-long ritual that purports to lead the practitioner to a powerful understanding of both angels and demons, making it one of the most influential grimoires in Western esotericism.

The Sworn Book of Honorius - This grimoire is an extension of the Grimoire of Pope Honorius and focuses on evocation and the summoning of both angels and demons. The text provides elaborate rituals to control and bind spirits, offering instructions on how to force demons to answer questions or fulfill certain tasks. It is often considered a "dangerous" grimoire because of the power it offers the practitioner over malevolent forces.

Known for its occult practices, The Black Pullet is a grimoire associated with talismans and the creation of magical objects. It contains detailed instructions for summoning spirits and demons, along with descriptions of their specific functions in magical workings. Unlike other grimoires that focus on the direct evocation of demons, The Black Pullet also delves into the creation of magical amulets and talismans to control demonic forces indirectly.

The Book of the Sacred Magic of Abramelin the Mage - This is a lengthy and complex grimoire that describes the process of obtaining the magical knowledge required to summon both angels and demons. It is closely tied to the concept of the Holy Guardian Angel and is often seen as one of the most important works in Western occultism.

The grimoire's connection to demons lies in the necessity of mastering the demons in order to attain spiritual enlightenment, though its main focus is on the practitioner's relationship with their divine protector.

The Pseudomonarchia Daemonum - A compilation by Johann Weyer, this text is a catalog of demons and spirits, providing detailed descriptions of their attributes, powers, and how to summon them. The demons listed in Pseudomonarchia Daemonum correspond with those found in the Ars

Goetia, but Weyer takes a more clinical approach, often emphasizing their roles as symbolic figures or warnings against pride and excess.

The Key of Solomon (Clavicula Salomonis) - While the Key of Solomon is primarily concerned with angelic and celestial workings, it also touches on summoning spirits and demons. The grimoire is a foundational text in Western ceremonial magic, offering rituals and spells designed to invoke divine powers but also containing rites for controlling spirits that can sometimes be interpreted as demonic entities.

The fear of demons, deeply rooted in religious, cultural, and historical contexts, has been amplified by the grimoires that detail their nature, power, and dangerous influence. These texts not only provided detailed descriptions of the demons themselves but also emphasized their malevolent qualities and their potential to lead practitioners astray.

Many grimoires, such as The Lesser Key of Solomon and The Grand Grimoire, presented demons as powerful, rebellious beings who defied God and sought to lead humans into sin. This framing taps into the deeply ingrained theological fear that any force opposing divine order is inherently dangerous. The Ars Goetia in particular described demons not just as spirits to be controlled or used, but as tricksters or malevolent forces that could deceive, manipulate, or corrupt those who summoned them depicting them as agents of chaos and destruction contributed to their fearsome reputation.

Grimoires often included intricate rituals for summoning demons, which required specific tools, words of power, and often dangerous oaths. The Book of Abramelin and The Key of Solomon included steps for evoking spirits with the potential for personal empowerment, but also laid out detailed warnings of the risks involved. The fear of being unprepared or unknowingly unleashing a demon (or the fear of being controlled by them) became a significant part of the cultural narrative around these texts. Practitioners were warned that they could lose their soul or sanity if they failed in these rites.

These books, especially during the Christianization of Europe, contributed to the fear of demons by demonizing pre-Christian deities and spirits. Gods once revered in ancient cultures were recast as demons, which helped align Christian cosmology against any form of non-Christian spirituality. For instance, the Roman god Pan, associated with nature and fertility, became equated with the Devil in Christian iconography. This rebranding of pagan deities as demonic forces fueled the idea that certain forms of worship, magic, and spiritual practice were not just wrong but dangerous and evil.

The fear of demons was also tied to the broader Christian notion of Hell and eternal damnation. Grimoires like the Grand Grimoire and The Pseudomonarchia Daemonum often linked demons to the underworld, portraying them as agents of torment and suffering. This view was closely aligned with the fear of spiritual corruption and eternal punishment, which was heavily emphasized in the medieval Christian world. Such associations amplified the belief that working with demons could lead to a loss of salvation or a descent into damnation.

The theme of the grimoires is the demon's role as a corrupter of souls. For example, the Grand Grimoire and The Black Pullet often describe pacts with demons as a way to gain wealth, power, or forbidden knowledge. However, these gains are presented as temporary and ultimately destructive, leading to spiritual decay. The focus on tempting humans with worldly desires, only to trap them in the process, reinforces the view that demons are dangerous because they prey on human weakness.

The grimoires and demonology was not just a spiritual or theological one but also a psychological and cultural phenomenon. The more detailed the grimoires became in describing the power and influence of demons, the more ingrained these fears became in the collective consciousness. This led to widespread superstition, witch hunts, and the societal condemnation of those perceived to be practicing forbidden magic. People feared demons not only for their power over the physical world but for their ability to manipulate human emotions, desires, and actions .

King, Prince, or President? - The Meaning Behind the Title

As we move from the historical texts and grimoires into a more practical and symbolic understanding of demonology, it's important to explore one often-overlooked yet powerful aspect of working with demons: their titles. These roles—King, Lord, Prince, Duke, and so on—may seem like medieval leftovers or theatrical embellishments, but within magical systems, titles carry weight. They signal not only the demon's place in the infernal hierarchy but also offer insight into the kind of power, domain, and relationship the spirit holds.

By examining these titles, we begin to uncover a deeper structure within the world of spirits—one that mirrors the hierarchies of earthly empires, yet also transcends them, reflecting cosmic principles, elemental forces, and archetypal truths. Reclaiming this understanding allows us to see beyond the fear-based interpretations of demons as mere agents of chaos. Instead, we recognize them as beings embedded in complex systems of wisdom, authority, and transformation.

The hierarchical structure presented in texts like the Ars Goetia was heavily influenced by medieval and Renaissance worldviews, especially the blending of celestial orders with feudal ideals. This was not accidental—occultists of the time saw the spiritual world as a mirror of the physical one. Just as a kingdom had its nobles and rulers, so too did the spiritual realms.

The title of King denotes the highest authority within infernal ranks. Kings command vast legions and often possess dominion over entire regions of the infernal plane or over grand human domains—such as empire, conquest, or the primal forces of nature. Kings are beings of immense power and often carry ancient wisdom or dominion over life-altering forces. Asmodeus, Paimon, and Bael are frequently listed as kings, each with their own unique associations—pleasure, knowledge, command, and more.

A Lord is often a more fluid title, not always present in the classic grimoires but appearing in modern interpretations and personal gnosis. Lords typically wield authority within a specific realm or concept—such as war, death, or initiation. Azazel, for instance, is often called a Lord, particularly within modern paths of demonolatry and left-hand practice. The title emphasizes sovereignty and mastery, but not necessarily universal rulership. Lords are often approached when one seeks transformation through trial or the unlocking of ancient, often taboo, knowledge.

Princes are usually ranked just below Kings and are often granted authority by a higher entity—sometimes Lucifer, sometimes another sovereign spirit. Their dominion may be more specialized, governing over aspects of human life such as diplomacy, love, or destruction. The Prince of Darkness, a title often given to Satan, reflects this concept of delegated, yet formidable, authority. Princes often act as intermediaries between practitioners and more supreme powers, making them ideal spirits for those working toward greater mastery or personal elevation.

A Duke is typically a commander of a specific legion and is often associated with focused domains such as healing, moral philosophy, science, or elemental control. Buer, for instance, is listed as a Duke in the Ars Goetia and is said to govern knowledge of natural and moral philosophy, as well as healing.

Dukes are approachable spirits for targeted workings—whether for insight, change, or mastery over a specific challenge.

Though a somewhat modern-sounding title, President appears in traditional grimoires like the Ars Goetia and denotes a being with organizational, intellectual, or social power. Presidents are frequently invoked for their ability to influence systems—political, intellectual, or personal. They are administrators, skilled in strategy, rhetoric, and guidance. They are often invoked for clarity in communication or influence in leadership roles.

Marquis, Count, and Earl: These titles generally denote mid-tier spirits, often with particular niches or temperaments. A Marquis may oversee territorial or psychological domains and often engages with transformation or disruption—Amon being a prime example, known for revealing the past and reconciling friendships. Counts and Earls represent lower-ranking spirits but are no less powerful within their assigned functions. They may offer support in very specific magical workings, such as protection, uncovering secrets, or resolving inner conflicts.

Understanding these titles is more than a historical exercise. It helps us align our intent with the right spiritual ally. In magic, names and roles are not arbitrary—they are vessels of meaning and channels of connection. Recognizing a demon's title can shape how we approach them, what kind of relationship we build, and the type of wisdom we seek to uncover. These ranks speak not only to their power, but to their role in the soul's journey—offering guidance, transformation, or challenge depending on what the practitioner is ready to receive.

Hierarchy and Influence Within the Infernal Pantheon

The titles given to demons do more than suggest rank—they form a symbolic architecture that reflects the flow of power, influence, and cosmic function within the infernal pantheon. These hierarchies mirror the social and political structures familiar to the cultures that shaped them, but they also encode deeper esoteric truths. A King or a Duke in these systems is not simply a ruler or military commander, but a spirit whose domain intersects with specific currents of power in both the spiritual and human realms.

In texts like the *Ars Goetia* and *Malleus Maleficarum*, the infernal realm is presented as an orderly kingdom with designated roles and responsibilities. These writings often depict demons not merely as chaotic forces, but as functionaries within a broader cosmic system—tempters, punishers, teachers, and guides. Their titles delineate spheres of influence: some govern wide domains like knowledge, war, or lust, while others work more subtly, presiding over personal transformation, hidden insight, or elemental forces.

These hierarchical titles emerge from a fusion of Christian theology and earlier pagan belief systems. In ancient pantheons, gods and spirits held dominion over natural elements, human experiences, and metaphysical principles. As Christianity expanded, many of these deities were rebranded as demons, their old titles preserved but reinterpreted.

The Church, reflecting the feudal structure of its own time, cast these beings as rebellious nobles in a cosmic war—kings and princes in exile, fallen but still formidable.

Thus, the term *King* in demonology became not just a marker of power but a signifier of fallen grandeur—a ruler over shadowed realms rather than celestial heights. This inversion was intentional, reinforcing the narrative of divine order versus infernal rebellion. Yet within occult traditions, especially those that reject binary morality, these titles reclaim their complexity. A *Prince* of Hell may not be a corrupter but a challenger of stagnant systems. A *Lord* may be a guardian of secret knowledge.

In the Western esoteric worldview, the universe is composed of interwoven opposites—light and shadow, order and chaos, ascent and descent. Demonic hierarchies reflect this balance. They are not just symbols of corruption, but of change, transformation, and necessary disruption. Lucifer, often seen as the archetypal rebel, becomes a symbol of personal enlightenment and evolution—an agent of divine spark through defiance.

Just as angels are considered messengers and enforcers of divine law, demons can be viewed as enforcers of natural and spiritual laws that are more primal, less tame. Many govern forces that are deeply human and powerfully transformative: desire, decay, ambition, fear, destruction, sex, and renewal. In this sense, their work is not to oppose divine will, but to enact it in its more chaotic, catalytic forms.

Higher-ranking demons are often invoked for major workings—initiations, the pursuit of power, deep knowledge—while lower-ranking spirits are approached for practical needs, guidance, or emotional work. Yet all levels of the hierarchy serve a purpose. The interplay between them reflects the movement of energy and intention across both the mundane and spiritual planes. These titles help practitioners navigate the spirit world with intention and clarity, aligning their needs with the appropriate spirit's domain.

Understanding the infernal hierarchy is not merely about organizing spirits into ranks—it is a way of mapping the practitioner's own spiritual path. These spirits offer mirrors for our ambitions, our darkness, our longing to transcend limits. Through them, we interact with the forces that shape not only our outer world, but our inner alchemy.

Ultimately, the demonic hierarchy is a living system. Its structure is not fixed by dogma, but shaped by centuries of myth, magic, and personal gnosis. For practitioners today, it offers a framework for understanding the cosmos and one's place within it. It provides not just names and ranks, but a vision of spiritual ecology where every force—no matter how feared or revered—has its role in the greater balance.

12. Working With Demons

Deity work refers to spiritual practices in which a practitioner connects with, honors, and seeks guidance from a specific deity or pantheon. These practices vary widely depending on tradition, belief system, or personal spiritual approach. They are found in ancient religions—such as those of Greece, Egypt, or the Norse peoples—as well as in modern witchcraft, paganism, and mysticism.

At its core, deity work is about relationship. Practitioners might offer devotion, create sacred space, and engage in prayer, meditation, or ritual to build a bond with a deity. This connection can range from formal worship to a more personal or reciprocal dynamic, where the deity is experienced as a guide, teacher, or ally.

Offerings—such as food, incense, candles, or symbolic items—are common and serve as a gesture of respect, gratitude, or invitation. Many practitioners set up altars or sacred spaces that reflect the deity's nature, adorned with images, symbols, or tools associated with them. These spaces become centers for reflection, communion, and transformation.

Deity work is often undertaken to receive insight, guidance, healing, or empowerment. Through consistent practice, many seek to embody the virtues or energies of the deity they honor—whether strength, wisdom, love, or justice. This same framework can be applied to working with demons.

In this chapter, we will explore what it means to approach demons not as threats, but as ancient spiritual forces—teachers, allies, or mirrors of our inner world. Drawing on alchemy, astrology, and occult philosophy, we will begin to uncover the deeper personalities and purposes of these entities. Through this exploration, you'll learn how to incorporate them into your personal practice—whether through ritual, meditation, altar work, or direct communication—and discover how their energies might guide, challenge, or empower you on your spiritual path.

DEMONS AND PLANETARY ARCHETYPES IN OCCULT TRADITIONS

In many occult systems, demons are not merely chaotic or malevolent entities, but deeply symbolic beings—archetypal forces intricately connected to the greater fabric of the cosmos. One of the most enduring frameworks for understanding their nature lies in their correlation with planetary archetypes. Just as the planets in astrology represent distinct currents of influence—such as communication, power, transformation, and discipline—so too do the demons associated with them embody these qualities in potent, often shadowed forms.

This correspondence between demons and planetary forces appears across grimoires, magical systems, and esoteric philosophies. It offers a lens through which practitioners can better understand the energies at play when engaging with these entities, and more importantly, how to work with them in intentional, transformative ways.

I will use Azazel's connection to Saturn to explain this more thoroughly. Saturn governs boundaries, discipline, structure, karma, and the lessons of time. In astrology, it is the planet of hardship, but also of profound wisdom earned through struggle. Azazel, as mentioned, a fallen angel and the bearer of forbidden knowledge, embodies Saturn's stern, transformative nature. Working with Azazel can mean confronting one's fears, limitations, and internal darkness. He is a teacher of responsibility, autonomy, and strength gained through adversity. His wisdom is not comforting, but it is enduring—offering the practitioner an uncompromising mirror through which they can refine themselves.

Saturn is also a planet of spiritual authority and cosmic justice. Azazel's role in challenging the status quo and delivering knowledge that breaks oppressive structures aligns with this current. He offers liberation not through indulgence, but through mastery.

Demons aligned with Mars—such as Asmodeus—carry the volatile fire of desire, courage, aggression, and raw willpower. Mars is the blade, the battlefield, the lustful cry of life striving to conquer or be conquered. These demons can help the practitioner cut through fear, initiate action, and embrace the primal aspects of passion—whether in battle, love, or self-assertion. Rituals aligned with Mars may be used for protection, conflict resolution, breaking through stagnation, or reclaiming one's personal power in times of adversity.

The planet Venus governs love, beauty, seduction, and attraction. Demons connected to Venus, such as Lilith, reflect not only the enchantment of desire but also the power of self-liberation through sensuality. Lilith embodies the darker, untamed aspects of Venus—the sacred rage and erotic rebellion against oppression.

To work with Venus-aligned demons is to explore the relationship between beauty and power, autonomy and pleasure. These spirits often help in work related to self-love, attraction, artistic inspiration, or sexual empowerment.

Mercury, planet of intellect, communication, and movement, resonates with demons like Paimon, who are known for their eloquence, cunning, and wisdom. These spirits guide practitioners in the realms of study, negotiation, divination, and persuasion. They are ideal allies in work involving contracts, speech, clever problem-solving, and the uncovering of hidden knowledge. Their trickster nature reminds us that all wisdom comes at a cost—and that the truth is often layered and complex.

Jupiter governs growth, prosperity, leadership, and sacred law. Demons associated with Jupiter—such as Baal or Baphomet—often represent power, rulership, and the mysteries of transformation through spiritual expansion. These spirits are useful in rituals for wealth, authority, learning, and gaining respect or recognition. They also govern esoteric truths, philosophical insight, and mastery over the self and others.

In magical practice, aligning ritual with planetary timing (planetary hours or days) can strengthen the results of your work. By invoking a demon through the lens of their planetary archetype, the practitioner amplifies the energy being called upon. For example:

- Saturn-aligned demons are best approached during Saturn hours for endurance, shadow work, or long-term goals.

- Mars-aligned demons may be called upon for bold action, protection, or dealing with rage.

- Venus-aligned demons suit love spells, beauty rituals, or reclamation of desire.

- Mercury spirits guide intellectual pursuits, creative writing, divination, and cunning.

- Jupiter demons are potent allies in career advancement, abundance work, or spiritual leadership.

Each planetary archetype offers unique gifts—and challenges. The demon aligned with that planet becomes the gatekeeper to that realm of experience.

In conclusion, the connection between demons and planetary archetypes is not just symbolic—it's functional. It provides a map, a system of correspondences that can be used to deepen spiritual work and create more effective rituals. By understanding these planetary qualities, the practitioner gains greater clarity on which demon to approach, how to work with them, and what results to expect.

These spirits are not simply embodiments of chaos—they are mirrors of the cosmos, reflecting back to us the archetypal forces that shape both the outer universe and our inner world.

The Alchemy of Demons

Demons often have strong connections to the classical elements: Earth, Fire, Air, and Water. These elements represent the foundational forces of nature in many ancient philosophies, and demons associated with them embody the traits and qualities of these natural powers. The relationship between demons and the elements plays a crucial role in their influence and the types of energies they can invoke in a practitioner's life. Understanding these associations can provide deeper insight into the nature of these entities and how they might assist in magical workings.

The Earth element is traditionally connected to stability, grounding, material wealth, and physical manifestation. Demons tied to Earth tend to be associated with matters of the body, the material world, and prosperity.

Baal, Belial and Baphomet are a few examples of demons associated with Earth due to their power over the material world and the ability to bestow wealth, influence, and fertility. Earth-bound demons like these are often invoked for material success, physical strength, or protection. Demons linked to Earth are also thought to help with issues related to endurance, patience, and overcoming obstacles. They may assist in bringing about success in business, personal development, or even legal matters. Their energy is slow-moving and requires long-term commitment, much like the enduring force of the Earth itself.

The Fire element represents energy, transformation, action, and destruction. Fire is a highly dynamic force, symbolizing both creation and destruction, and is often tied to demons that govern transformation, change, and personal power. Demons associated with Fire are often invoked for their ability to ignite passion, overcome fears, or bring about powerful transformations in the practitioner's life. Asmodeus, a demon often associated with lust and desire, is linked to the Fire element due to his connection to intense passions, both destructive and creative. Fire demons can stimulate change, both by burning away the old and lighting the path to something new. Fire demons can inspire ambition, drive, and personal growth. Their energy is best used for breaking through limitations, sparking creativity, and motivating action. They are ideal for practitioners looking to make bold changes or take strong action in their lives.

Air represents the mental realm—intellect, communication, and creativity. Demons connected to Air are thought to have dominion over thoughts, knowledge, and verbal expression. They are invoked for their ability to stimulate the mind, enhance communication skills, or assist in creative endeavors. Paimon, a demon known for his vast knowledge and intellect, is often associated with the Air element. He is a teacher and guide in the occult, and his influence over the mental realm makes him a powerful figure for enhancing one's intellectual abilities, learning, and even divination. Air demons assist with intellectual pursuits, the expansion of knowledge, and improving one's ability to communicate and express ideas. They can help open the mind to new possibilities and are often invoked in rituals that involve divination, spellcasting, or seeking higher wisdom.

Water is the element of emotions, intuition, and the subconscious. It is fluid, adaptable, and deeply connected to the unseen forces that shape our internal world. Demons tied to Water are often associated with emotional healing, psychic abilities, and the flow of intuition. Astaroth, who is sometimes depicted as a demon of knowledge and transformation, is associated with Water. They can guide individuals in emotional healing, self-discovery, and spiritual growth, encouraging introspection and the exploration of hidden aspects of the self. Demons linked to Water are valuable for rituals aimed at emotional release, self-healing, and accessing hidden knowledge within the subconscious mind. They can aid in purging negative emotions, improving psychic awareness, and nurturing deep spiritual growth.

The key to working with the elemental aspect of demons lies in understanding how their unique qualities align with the practitioner's goals. Invoking a demon of Fire for passion and change might be appropriate when one is seeking to bring swift transformation. Conversely, invoking a demon of Earth could be beneficial when grounded, material success is the focus.

By tailoring rituals to align with elemental energies, practitioners can unlock the full potential of these demonic forces, guiding them to work in harmony with nature's elements and their own desires.

With that said, you can also use that knowledge to give offerings connected to their element, ask the demon to amplify your fire magick or draw from the element itself. It can also help you recognize their unique energetic signature.

In summary, demons' connections to the elements offer a framework for understanding their influence over different aspects of life, from material gain and protection (Earth) to transformation (Fire), knowledge (Air), and emotional healing (Water). Each element brings its own energy and essence, providing practitioners with a variety of tools for spiritual work, personal empowerment, and magical success. But there is also the connection between demons and alchemical elements, such as iron, gold, and lead for the practitioner to explore.

In alchemy, each metal and mineral is often associated with specific spiritual or energetic qualities, and certain demons are linked to these materials as representations of transformation, power, and elemental influence.

The alchemical tradition often associates specific metals with particular spiritual properties, and demons, as symbolic forces or guides, can also be connected to these metals based on their qualities, roles, and the transformation they facilitate.

Copper is often associated with the planet Venus and symbolizes beauty, love, harmony, and creativity. In alchemy, copper is linked to the principle of attraction and unity, often representing the female aspect of creation. Demons like Asmodeus, the demon of lust and passion, are often connected with copper due to the metal's symbolic relationship with love, desire, and sensuality. Copper's bright, reddish hue aligns with the fiery and passionate qualities that Asmodeus represents, particularly in how desire can be both a source of personal growth and personal excess. Copper can be used in spiritual workings related to love, creativity, and fertility. For example, invoking Asmodeus with copper could be aimed at enhancing passion or creativity in art, relationships, and desires.

Silver is linked to the moon and represents intuition, reflection, and the subconscious mind. It is the metal of the feminine divine and symbolizes purity and clarity. Lilith, a demoness often linked with the moon and feminine power, is associated with silver. She embodies aspects of independence, intuition, and the untapped power of the shadow self, which is reflected in the properties of silver. Silver can be used in rituals for psychic development, intuition, and dreams. A practitioner seeking to enhance their inner wisdom might use silver and invoke Lilith for guidance in uncovering hidden truths or tapping into deeper emotional or spiritual wisdom.

Tin is traditionally associated with Jupiter, the planet of expansion, wisdom, and abundance. In alchemy, it signifies abundance, growth, and the elevation of consciousness. Paimon, a king among the demons in the Ars Goetia, is often connected with tin due to his role in offering knowledge, power, and influence, aligning with the expansive qualities of Jupiter. Paimon can help guide practitioners toward spiritual growth, wealth, and success. Tin could be used in rituals to seek spiritual growth, higher wisdom, or abundance in both material and spiritual life. Invoking Paimon while working with tin might help a practitioner open doors to new opportunities or enhance their leadership and influence.

Mercury (also known as quicksilver) is perhaps the most important alchemical metal. It represents fluidity, change, and transformation. It is the metal of duality—both a physical and spiritual element of balance and transition. Hermes, although more often considered a god, is sometimes represented as a demonic figure in some occult systems due to his association with knowledge, communication, and transformation. Buer, from the Ars Goetia, can also be linked to mercury due to his ability to facilitate healing and transformation. Mercury is commonly used in alchemical practices focused on transformation and change, particularly when one seeks to change mental or emotional states. Working with Buer and mercury could be helpful in healing, overcoming obstacles, and spiritual development.

Be mindful that mercury is a heavy metal that can be toxic to humans and animals, even in small amounts.

Gold is the most exalted metal in alchemical traditions, representing perfection, enlightenment, and spiritual illumination. It corresponds to the Sun and signifies the end goal of alchemical work: the Philosopher's Stone, which grants eternal life and enlightenment. Lucifer, as the light-bringer, is often associated with gold. His role as a bearer of knowledge and illumination is reflected in gold's association with wisdom, power, and spiritual ascent. Gold represents the height of human achievement, symbolizing the path to spiritual enlightenment and mastery over the material world. Gold is often used in rituals for enlightenment, manifestation, and the pursuit of higher wisdom. Invoking Lucifer while working with gold can be a way to seek intellectual clarity, spiritual insight, and personal transformation.

Lead is the metal most often associated with the beginning stages of alchemy. It represents the base, unrefined state of being that must undergo purification and transmutation into something greater—like gold. Lead symbolizes challenges, hardships, and the necessary trials to achieve spiritual refinement. Saturn, and the demon Zagan, is associated with lead, as Saturn he governs time, discipline, structure, and necessary suffering. Demons associated with this planet often represent the lessons learned through adversity and the necessary work required to achieve spiritual mastery. Lead can be used in rituals focused on overcoming hardship, purification, and learning from life's challenges. Invoking Zagan can help one work through difficulties, purify the soul, and understand deeper truths.

Steel is a more refined version of iron and represents strength, protection, and the fortification of one's will. It is a symbol of the warrior's journey and the mental clarity needed to overcome conflict. Aamon, a demon associated with vengeance, war, and conflict, can be linked to steel. Steel's sharpness and strength correspond to Aamon's role in assisting those who need to protect themselves or achieve victory in battle. Steel can be used in rituals for protection, to bolster one's willpower, or to confront inner and outer conflicts. Aamon's influence may be called upon when seeking victory over adversaries or to fortify oneself against negative forces.

These metals are not just physical substances but hold significant esoteric meanings in alchemical traditions. They align with the transformative, spiritual work that demons facilitate, where the materials themselves become symbols for inner growth, challenges, and achievements.

Demons connected to these metals can guide practitioners on a journey of self-transformation, each metal offering a unique energy to work with, whether for protection, enlightenment, healing, or power. Let us use Azazel as an example on how to use alchemy in our practice and in understanding these entities on a deeper level.

Azazel's connection to iron is notable in some occult traditions, particularly given his role in teaching forbidden knowledge to humanity, such as the art of warfare and the crafting of weapons. Iron, in alchemy, is a symbol of resilience, strength, and transformation. As the metal of Mars, the god of war, iron aligns with Azazel's role in imparting knowledge of combat and material force. This could suggest that Azazel's energies assist in overcoming inner battles, forging spiritual strength through trials, and transforming the practitioner's will and endurance. Iron's association with purification in alchemical practices parallels Azazel's work of guiding the practitioner through dark, challenging times toward self-mastery and empowerment.

Lead is traditionally seen as the starting point in the alchemical process—raw, unrefined, and base. It is associated with the necessary work of purging impurities before reaching spiritual perfection or enlightenment. I connect this to him being well-suited for the inexperienced practitioner.

Azazel's work in offering divine secrets to humankind mirrors the process of turning base materials into gold, symbolizing the refining of one's soul and gaining access to higher realms of knowledge. The fallen angel who defied divine order, can be seen as embodying the alchemical journey from darkness to light. In invoking Azazel, practitioners may seek to transmute their base desires, fears, or weaknesses (symbolized by lead) into wisdom and power (symbolized by gold). Azazel's teachings and influence can facilitate the internal transformation of negative traits, catalyzing a more profound understanding of self and spiritual awakening.

In the world of alchemy, transmutation — the shifting of one element into another — is seen as both a material process and a symbolic spiritual journey. Azazel's connection to the metals of iron, lead, and gold reflects the phases of alchemical purification and can be understood as the path he guides the practitioner through.

Iron (Base Power to Strength): Azazel's teachings of power and war correspond to the strength necessary to begin the alchemical process.

Lead (Purging of Impurities): Azazel helps practitioners face their shadow self and weaknesses, transmuting the lead of their darker sides into enlightenment.

Gold (Spiritual Illumination): Through the final stages of spiritual work, Azazel's knowledge and wisdom guide the practitioner toward enlightenment, symbolized by the alchemical gold.

Using alchemical symbolism is just one of many tools we can draw on to understand and connect with these entities.

Exploring Animal Archetypes in Demonology

The depiction of certain demons in the Ars Goetia as animals or part-animal likely stems from a combination of symbolic, cultural, and religious influences. These hybrid forms are not literal descriptions, but rather symbolic expressions that reflect deeper spiritual and psychological meanings—rooted in mythology, medieval occultism, and subconscious archetypes.

Animals in art and mythology often represent untamed instincts or natural forces—strength, cunning, lust, fear. When demons are described with animalistic features, these symbols express the primal energies they govern. A lion's head may signify ferocity and courage, while a serpent body suggests transformation, deception, or ancient wisdom.

As Christianity spread, many pagan deities and nature spirits—some already bearing animal forms—were reimagined as demons. Egyptian gods like Anubis, or Greek gods such as Pan, were depicted with animal traits that later became marks of the "infernal" in Christian demonology. Bael, described in the Ars Goetia with the heads of a toad, cat, and man, likely echoes ancient fertility and underworld deities, tied to cycles of life, death, and renewal.

The medieval European fascination with bestiaries—allegorical texts that assigned moral or spiritual symbolism to animals—also influenced how demons were portrayed. A snake became a symbol of sin; the lion, nobility; the dog, loyalty. These associations helped shape the visual and conceptual language used in grimoires to convey the nature of each demon.

Hybrid forms, combining human and animal, emphasize a demon's "otherness"—beings that exist beyond human comprehension and outside natural order. This echoes fears of losing control, surrendering to instinct, or confronting the unknown. Many of these depictions may also be rooted in dreamwork or mystical visions, where archetypal forms emerge from the subconscious to convey deeper truths.

Scriptural references also contributed to these hybrid portrayals. In the Book of Revelation, supernatural beings are described with lion, ox, eagle, and human aspects—beings of immense symbolic power. Satan's association with the serpent and dragon further influenced how demons were imagined: as beastly, ancient, and fearsome.

Pre-Christian animistic traditions saw nature spirits and chthonic beings as sacred and powerful. With Christianization, many of these entities were demonized, their animalistic aspects reframed as signs of corruption or chaos. The grotesque imagery served to instill fear, but it also preserved the raw spiritual potency these beings once commanded.

As witches and demonolaters, we understand that these animal features are not merely monstrous but meaningful. They are archetypal keys— clues to the deeper character and influence of a demon. They can guide us in understanding how a demon operates energetically, what lessons it may teach, and how best to approach it in ritual or meditation. Take Azazel, for example. His association with the goat traces back to the scapegoat ritual described in Leviticus, where one goat was sacrificed and the other sent into the wilderness "to Azazel," bearing the sins of the people.

Over time, the goat became a symbol of both sin and sovereignty—of exile and freedom. Esoterically, the goat represents vitality, independence, and wild, untamed wisdom. Azazel, through this symbol, embodies both sacrifice and rebellion, making him a powerful figure in initiatory shadow work.

Asmodeus is often linked with the bull, a universal symbol of lust, strength, and fertility. The bull's virility reflects Asmodeus's role in stirring desire, but also in channeling passion into personal power. Its connection to raw physical force makes it an appropriate symbol for grounding one's will and overcoming inhibition.

Stolas is described in the Goetia as appearing in the form of an owl, a creature of mystery, moonlight, and hidden knowledge. The owl is a traditional symbol of wisdom, intuition, and the unseen—aligning with Stolas's role as a teacher of astronomy, plants, and precious stones. His nocturnal symbolism makes him a guide for those exploring the mysteries of the occult or developing psychic abilities.

Beelzebub, known as the "Lord of the Flies," reflects the fly's symbolism of decay, corruption, and the thin veil between life and death. It is a reminder of impermanence—and a mirror for confronting what festers in the shadow.

Leviathan, the great sea serpent, represents chaos, the deep unconscious, and the abyss of primordial waters. It is the raw, undifferentiated source from which all emotion and creativity emerge—and in its depths, the practitioner may face both terror and transformation.

Amon, in some traditions, is associated with the wolf—a figure that embodies both predation and loyalty. The wolf walks the line between civilization and the wild, making it an ideal symbol for a demon who deals in duality, strategy, and conflict.

These symbolic animals serve as more than metaphor—they are spiritual tools, meditative focal points, and living archetypes. The goat can teach us about duality and responsibility. The owl opens our inner sight. The bull grounds us in physical strength and vitality. Through these symbols, the practitioner is invited to not only understand the demon, but also connect with its domain through offerings, visualizations, or animal-based correspondences in ritual.

These archetypes also encourage deep introspection. What within you is wild, hidden, instinctual, or feared? As with the demons they represent, these animals can become guides through the underworld of the self—helping you confront your shadows, awaken your power, and claim your spiritual autonomy.

By working with these animal symbols in mindful ways, you deepen your relationship with the demon and open new doorways within yourself. This integration of myth, symbol, and spirit transforms your practice from invocation into communion—bridging the realms of the natural and the divine.

Dictionare Infernal illustration of Bael

Deity Work within the Infernal Pantheon

Deity work with demons differs significantly from working with gods and goddesses in traditional pantheons. In established systems such as those of Ancient Greece, Egypt, or Hinduism, deities are often regarded as divine forces presiding over specific aspects of nature, the cosmos, or human experience. These gods are typically approached through structured rituals, prayers, and offerings intended to gain blessings, guidance, or protection. The relationship is often one of reverence, devotion, and alignment with divine order.

Across cultures and traditions, deity work manifests in unique ways. Ancient Greeks made offerings to deities like Athena or Apollo for wisdom or protection. Egyptian rituals honored gods like Isis and Osiris through sacred oils, incense, and prayers. Hindu devotion includes puja ceremonies, bhajans (devotional songs), and offerings of fruit or flowers to gods like Lakshmi or Shiva. In modern Wicca and neo-pagan paths, deity work might involve seasonal rituals, creative offerings, and invocations to deities like Hecate, Pan, or Brigid. In shamanic practices, deity work can include spirit journeys and ancestral communication, connecting the practitioner to divine or elemental forces through trance and ritual.

Deity work is often devotional, seeking harmony with the divine, blessings, or embodiment of certain virtues. But it can also be co-creative—a deeply personal relationship where the practitioner works alongside the deity for healing, insight, or transformation.

In contrast, demons invite a very different kind of relationship. The infernal pantheon lacks the formalized worship systems seen in traditional religions. Instead, working with demons often requires practitioners to forge their own path—crafting rituals, invocations, and offerings based on direct experience, intuition, and personal revelation.

This individualized approach is both liberating and demanding. It offers flexibility and autonomy but also places responsibility on the practitioner to build meaningful, respectful relationships. Some works, like The Complete Book of Demonolatry by S. Connolly, provide frameworks for working with demons, and Connolly's influence has helped shape modern demonolatry as both a spiritual path and, for some, a religious practice.

However, many practitioners—including myself—do not see demonolatry as a religion, but rather as a form of spiritual partnership and self-development. This is not about blind worship. Instead, it is about engaging with beings who challenge us, who reveal truths we might rather avoid, and who push us to evolve.

Where gods may offer harmony and protection, demons often present confrontation, transformation, and the dismantling of illusions. They do not hand out blessings freely; they demand effort, honesty, and inner work.

Importantly, the term demon encompasses a vast array of entities. Some may behave like deities—offering protection, wisdom, and structured guidance. Others resist worship altogether, preferring mutual respect or even adversarial challenge. A demon like Lucifer, for example, might be approached as a teacher or a divine spark—worthy of reverence but not control. Others, particularly those associated with rebellion or disruption, may demand autonomy and prefer to act as catalysts rather than caretakers.

This diversity makes it essential to approach each demon as an individual. There is no one-size-fits-all method. Some demons welcome offerings, others do not care. Some respond to formal invocations, others prefer spontaneous interaction. The key is relationship—built on trust, patience, and attentive listening.

In this book, I focus on a few select demons—especially Azazel, with whom I have a personal bond. These examples are not meant to speak for all demons, but rather to illustrate how deep, meaningful connections can develop over time. The goal is not to generalize, but to show how personalized, respectful approaches can lead to powerful partnerships.

Invocation, Evocation, Worship, and Shadow Work

As you begin your own journey, one of the first concepts you'll encounter is Invocation—a central technique in deity and demon work alike.

Invocation involves drawing a demon or deity inward—into one's body, consciousness, or energetic field. It is an immersive experience where the practitioner seeks a direct connection, allowing the entity's presence to move through them. This form of deity work often leads to personal transformation, insight, or a temporary merging of energies. Invocation is intimate, intense, and usually performed in a sacred space with preparation, focus, and consent.

Evocation, by contrast, is the act of summoning a demon or deity into a designated ritual space—externally rather than internally. The practitioner calls the entity's presence into the room, temple, or circle in order to communicate, seek assistance, or direct magical workings such as divination, protection, or transformation. Unlike invocation, evocation does not involve channeling the entity's energy through the self. It is often viewed as more formal, sometimes even commanding—though in modern occult practice, respectful consent and clear intention are emphasized to avoid treating the demon as a tool rather than a conscious being. Evocation creates a space for dialogue and cooperation rather than merging.

Worship, in the context of deity work, goes beyond interaction and becomes a devotional act. This may include structured rituals, offerings, prayers, or full ceremonies dedicated to honoring the entity's power, guidance, or influence. Worship is not always transactional—it can be done without asking for anything in return. Rather, it's about recognizing and revering the divine essence of the entity, much like one would a god or goddess. Worship may take the form of regular practices, feast days, altars, songs, or life rituals that express loyalty, respect, and gratitude.

Some demons appreciate worship. Others reject it. This is why developing a relationship with the demon in question—getting to know their preferences, their nature, and their energy—is essential. Not all spirits desire the same kind of engagement, and not all relationships are built on veneration. Some are founded on mutual challenge and growth.

Shadow Work is another profound dimension of deity or demon work. Rooted in Jungian psychology, shadow work involves confronting and integrating the hidden, repressed, or wounded parts of the self—those aspects we deny, fear, or feel ashamed of. Demons are particularly potent allies in this work because they embody the liminal, the forbidden, the raw, and the rejected. Their very nature invites us to look into the dark and find power where we were taught to feel shame.

In this context, a demon might not be a tormentor, but a mirror. Not a corrupter, but a catalyst. Through working with demons in shadow work, practitioners are encouraged to embrace uncomfortable truths, dismantle harmful beliefs, and emerge stronger and more whole. These spirits do not demand moral perfection—they demand authenticity, accountability, and the courage to evolve.

Whether your path involves invocation, evocation, worship, or shadow work, each approach offers a unique gateway to spiritual insight and transformation. There is no singular "right way" to work with demons—only the path that resonates most deeply with your practice, your intention, and your truth.

Sigils - Origins and Occult Significance

The term sigil comes from the Latin sigillum, meaning "seal." Historically, sigils were symbols used to represent spiritual entities, often found in grimoires and magical texts, where they functioned as visual identifiers and conduits of magical power.

In the medieval and Renaissance eras, sigils became prominent in Solomonic magic—particularly in texts like The Lesser Key of Solomon (especially the Ars Goetia). These sigils were said to be the official seals of demons, used to summon, bind, or command them during ritual. The magician would draw the demon's sigil, often within a triangle or circle, as part of a highly structured invocation process. These were designed under the assumption that spirits needed to be compelled into obedience. But this is only one lens through which sigils can be viewed.

From a non-Solomonic perspective, sigils are not tools of control—but keys of communication. Rather than forcing a demon to appear, the sigil is seen as a personal symbol or energetic signature of the demon. When meditated upon, drawn, or empowered, the sigil attunes the practitioner, the offering or the spell to the spirit's presence. It's a point of resonance—like tuning into a specific frequency or spiritual current.

In modern magical systems—especially those rooted in chaos magic or witchcraft—sigils also became personalized magical symbols created by the practitioner to encode intent. Though not directly related to demonology, this trend reflects the enduring belief in symbols as tools to bypass the conscious mind and communicate with deeper spiritual or subconscious forces.

Over the years, I've encountered many practitioners who emphasize the importance of **not** drawing a circle around a demon's sigil, explaining that the circle symbolize binding or restraint. This caution often extends to jewelry, where the circle is a common and prominent design element.

As an artist, however, I see the circle around a sigil as a beautiful complement. It's important to remember that without the intention of binding, a circle is simply that: ornamental. If you find it beautiful, there is nothing inherently bad, evil, or disrespectful about it.

Some might argue that using the circle is inappropriate because historically it was intended as a means of control. But once again, it all comes down to intention. When approached with love and respect, incorporating the circle can even be seen as an act of gentle rebellion — a reclaiming of a symbol once meant for domination, transforming it instead into something honoring, expressive, and beautiful.

Enns - Mysterious Mantras of Connection

Enns are short, chanted phrases associated with specific demons—usually found in modern demonolatry, especially within the tradition influenced by the work of S. Connolly and the Demonolatry Clergy Association. These phrases are believed to help focus the mind, open spiritual gateways, and align the practitioner with the energy of the demon being called.

Unlike ancient languages like Hebrew or Latin used in ceremonial grimoires, enns are often written in a language referred to as "the demonic tongue," though its true origin is unclear. Some believe enns were received through gnosis or channeled experiences, rather than passed down from historical texts. While they do not appear in earlier grimoires like the Goetia, many practitioners report strong energetic experiences when using them—suggesting that their power may come from repetition, intention, and spiritual resonance, rather than historical roots.

An example of an enn used to connect with Asmodeus, often repeated in meditation or ritual to attune to his energy:

"Ayer avage Aloren Asmodeus aken."

Demons and Free Will

The concept of demons having free will is both complex and deeply significant across spiritual, occult, and religious traditions. Rather than viewing demons as mindless agents of chaos or mere instruments of fate, this perspective recognizes them as autonomous beings—entities with intentions, desires, and sovereignty over their actions. This understanding dramatically reshapes how practitioners engage with them.

In many traditions, demons are not portrayed as static, one-dimensional forces, but as beings with distinct personalities, temperaments, and motives. In grimoires like The Lesser Key of Solomon and The Goetia, they are presented not as automatons, but as rulers, scholars, warriors, and spirits with specific domains and goals. Their roles suggest not servitude but choice—willful participation in cosmic, spiritual, or human affairs.

For example, in The Book of Enoch, the angels who descended to Earth—including Azazel—did so of their own accord. They chose to break divine law to share forbidden knowledge with humanity. This rebellion was not simply a punishment; it was an act of volition. Such stories imply that demons, as fallen angels or independent spirits, possess free will and are not merely executing divine or infernal commands.

Acknowledging demonic free will adds both depth and challenge to spiritual practice. Demons are not bound to obey your every request, nor do they function like spiritual vending machines. They may choose to help—or not. They may respond in ways that surprise, provoke, or teach rather than simply fulfill.

This autonomy is one reason many practitioners approach demon work with caution—or avoid it altogether. A demon's assistance is never guaranteed, and if a request is made without clarity or alignment, the outcome might be vastly different than expected. These beings may challenge your assumptions, question your motives, or push you in uncomfortable directions. But it is often through that discomfort that growth occurs.

One of the ways demons exercise free will is through pacts or contracts. Unlike servitor spirits or ancestors bound by lineage, demons are often approached as equals or sovereign allies. A pact, then, is a mutual agreement, not a command. It can be formal—written or ritualized—or more fluid and intuitive, but it must be entered with clarity, respect, and serious intent.

Because demons are autonomous, they may interpret vague terms differently than you intended—or deliver results in unexpected ways. This is why clarity is paramount. Clearly define what you seek, what you offer in return, and what the parameters of the relationship are. Some practitioners choose to time-limit pacts, leaving space to review or revise the terms later.

Historical precedent for these kinds of spiritual agreements can be found in ancient animistic and shamanic traditions, where humans negotiated with spirits for protection, fertility, wisdom, or power. In both Mesopotamian and Hellenic traditions, intermediary spirits (daimones) could bless or disrupt a person's life, and offerings were made to honor, appease, or secure their cooperation.

Beyond contracts and requests, developing a relationship is one of the most powerful—and respectful—ways to work with demons. Through regular offerings, journaling, meditation, or dream work, a sense of trust and familiarity can be cultivated. Over time, the demon comes to know your path, your growth, and your intent—and may choose to walk beside you, not as a servant, but as a guide, mentor, or challenger.

As with any relationship, consistency and honesty matter. Authentic engagement signals that you are not merely using the demon, but inviting them into your practice as a true spiritual ally. This kind of long-term connection fosters deeper transformation, far beyond one-off spells or simple requests. Demons often respect those who approach them with sincerity, discipline, and a strong sense of self. They will test you—but not necessarily to harm you. Often, their challenges are meant to push you beyond ego, beyond fear, beyond illusion—to strip you bare so you can rebuild from a place of truth.

Working with autonomous beings requires emotional and spiritual maturity. While demons may hold power, they should not hold power over you. Do not become dependent. Do not relinquish your agency. A powerful partnership is one where both sides are respected, boundaries are upheld, and the practitioner remains grounded in their own sovereignty.

You are responsible for your spiritual path. Demons may illuminate the road, but you are the one who must walk it. Clarity of intent, regular self-reflection, and ethical accountability are essential. Ask yourself:

- Are my goals rooted in truth, or ego?

- Am I seeking power, or purpose?

- Does this relationship serve my growth, or merely my desires?

By maintaining this awareness, you ensure that the demon's free will aligns with your evolution rather than working against it.

The free will of demons is both a challenge and a gift. It requires you to show up fully, with clear intent and open eyes. It means navigating ambiguity, embracing complexity, and letting go of the illusion of control. But in doing so, you invite real transformation—a spiritual path not paved in comfort, but in courage. By choosing to work with beings who have their own wills, you are not asking for blind obedience—you are seeking a partnership. One built not on subservience, but on mutual power, shared insight, and the sacred dance of shadow and light.

13. The Evolving Faces of Demons

As discussed in this book, throughout history, the beings we now call demons have undergone profound transformations, shaped by mythology, cultural shifts, and human perceptions. These entities, once revered as powerful gods or celestial beings, became reframed as demonic forces in an effort to consolidate religious authority or explain the origins of human suffering. But what if these transformations are not merely about how we see them? A question I've often asked myself is; what if these beings themselves are engaged in a process of evolution and growth, much like humanity?

As a practitioner, working with and researching these entities, I've noticed these shifts. It is something I have often reflected on—how do these shifts in history affect the demon itself? A question we might never find an answer to, but it is still an interesting thought. This is why I've chosen to use Gilbert Simondon's theory of individuation to aid me in an analysis of this subject. The perspective provides an intriguing lens to explore these changes. It is a philosophical framework, which emphasizes the constant evolution of identity through tension, relationships, and transformation, and may help us understand demons as dynamic, relational beings. Just as individuals grow through interactions with others and their environment, do these entities adapt and grow through their connections to humanity, cultural beliefs, and spiritual practices?

In this chapter, we will delve into how these forgotten gods and demons might embody this process of individuation. These entities are not merely agents of chaos or destruction, but active participants in the collective and individual journeys of those who engage with them. But bear in mind that this is my own reflection and interpretation, written to provide insights into how these beings may serve as archetypes, guides, or even mirrors for our own spiritual evolution.

By exploring the thought of demons as participants in an ongoing process of transformation, we gain a deeper appreciation for their symbolic and spiritual significance. This chapter aims to spark discussions on how these forgotten gods evolve alongside us, offering lessons not only in rebellion and freedom but also in growth, balance, and the enduring quest for meaning.

Gilbert Simondon, a French philosopher, developed a nuanced theory of **individuation**, which addresses how beings (individuals, objects, or entities) come into being and maintain their existence. His work diverges from traditional metaphysical views by focusing on the process of becoming, rather than treating entities as fixed and fully formed. An individual is not something fully formed from the start but emerges through interactions within a system or environment.

A key concept in Simondon's philosophy is **transduction**—the process by which an individual organizes and structures itself by resolving internal or external tensions. Transduction is central to how individuals adapt and evolve within their environments. In a crystal, a seed crystal initiates a transductive process where new layers of the crystal structure form as molecules align with its existing pattern.

Simondon emphasized that individuals do not exist in isolation. The process of individuation is always relational, involving the environment, other beings, and the pre-individual field. Human individuation is linked to social and collective individuation, suggesting that society and individuals co-evolve. His emphasis on relational individuation complements themes of deity work. The evolution of a practitioner's relationship with demonic entities and other Devine beings mirrors the individuation process. Both parties—human and entity—transform through interaction, with shared tensions (shadow work, spiritual growth, etc.), fostering mutual evolution. Which could be one of the reasons why deities and demons contacts humans in the first place. Why they want to engage in a relationship with us.

Simondon's theory of individuation provides an insightful framework for understanding the shift in how occult practitioners relate to demons. His philosophy emphasizes the dynamic process of becoming—a continuous negotiation of tension and transformation within systems, rather than the static identities often assigned to entities or concepts.

In many occult systems, demons are associated with forbidden knowledge, transformation, and rebellion. Contact with humans may allow them to act as intermediaries between the known and unknown, guiding practitioners in uncovering hidden truths. This process aligns with Simondon's view that individuation is not just a personal phenomenon but also a systemic. In this sense, demons contribute to a larger evolution of collective spiritual and esoteric systems by challenging established norms and catalyzing growth.

The myth of the Watchers teaching humans metallurgy and astrology in the *Book of Enoch* reflects a mutual transformation. The Watchers disrupt divine order, but humanity evolves technologically and spiritually as a result.

In occult practices, demons are often invoked to exchange energy or knowledge. From Simondon's perspective, this energy flow represents a dynamic process where both the human and the demonic entity contribute to and are transformed by the interaction. Demons, as archetypes of rebellion, transformation, and hidden wisdom, require human interaction to embody and fulfill their roles within the cosmic system. Humans, in turn, find meaning and guidance by engaging with these archetypes. Just as humans strive for spiritual evolution, demons might also be part of a broader ontological system where their engagement with humanity allows them to "move" within their own hierarchies or evolve their functions within the spiritual cosmos.

From Instrumentalization to Relationality

In traditional occult frameworks, demons were often treated as tools—forces to be summoned, controlled, and wielded for personal gain. This approach reflects a static understanding, where demons existed merely to serve the magician's will, their identity and purpose reduced to fixed roles within ritual systems. Simondon's theory of individuation offers a powerful counterpoint: instead of seeing beings as static or finished, he frames them as relational and evolving, constantly shaped by tension, interaction, and transformation.

In contemporary occult practice, a profound shift is occurring. Practitioners no longer see demons as archetypes to dominate, but as dynamic teachers, guides, and allies—beings with agency, depth, and the capacity for growth. This mirrors Simondon's idea of transduction, where entities transform through contact and co-evolve in relationship with others. In this view, spiritual work becomes relational, not transactional. The practitioner changes through the relationship—and so, perhaps, does the demon.

Whereas older traditions reduced demons to fixed categories—agents of temptation, chaos, or destruction—modern practitioners recognize their multifaceted, individuating nature. Consider how shadow work has recontextualized demons: rather than adversaries, they are now seen as mirrors of the unconscious, reflections of suppressed emotion, and catalysts for transformation. This reflects Simondon's belief that individuation is not isolated—it happens within a field of shared tension, where both individuals and collectives are shaped through interaction.

The earlier hierarchical approach—where magicians bound demons into submission—rests on a paradigm of domination and control. In contrast, Simondon's philosophy emphasizes relationship over hierarchy, proposing that true power emerges through mediation, not coercion. Modern demonology embraces this shift. Practitioners often emphasize consent, mutual understanding, and co-creation. For example, viewing Azazel as a teacher rather than a tempter transforms the interaction. It moves from a dynamic of control to one of partnership, where both parties bring something meaningful to the exchange. The demon is no longer a tool—it is a co-agent in the practitioner's individuation.

Tension is not the enemy in this model—it is the crucible of growth. Historically, demons were feared as agents of disruption. But from a Simondonian perspective, this disruption is exactly what catalyzes individuation. Chaos is not destruction for its own sake—it is the first stage of becoming.

Nowhere is this clearer than in the integration of demons into shadow work. Here, the practitioner is invited to confront their hidden aspects— the fears, wounds, and desires buried beneath the surface. The demon becomes a guide through the underworld of the psyche, not to punish, but to illuminate. They are not symbols of evil, but initiators of transformation.

Reframing Demonization Through Individuation

Simondon's theory also provides a unique lens through which we can view the historical demonization of deities. His philosophy tells us that individuation arises from crisis—when a system encounters imbalance or contradiction, transformation occurs. This framework can help us understand how powerful gods became feared demons.

In their original cultural contexts, figures like Baal, Ishtar, Pan, and others were embodiments of nature, sovereignty, love, war, and fertility. They were woven into the cultural and cosmological frameworks of their people—a "pre-individual" field of meaning and relationship. Their presence helped maintain the spiritual equilibrium of their time. But when monotheistic religions rose to power, a new system was introduced—one that required unity, singular divinity, and strict moral binaries. The older gods posed a threat to this emerging order. So, through the mechanism of scapegoating, they were cast out, re-individuated as demons—symbols of rebellion, lust, wildness, and danger. This was not erasure. It was transformation. The identity of these beings did not disappear—it was reframed. Their traits were not lost, only recoded. Fertility became lust. Power became pride. Wilderness became chaos. The divine became demonic.

And yet—they endured.

Even within their demonized forms, they continued to evolve, to speak, to beckon. Today, many practitioners return to these figures—reclaiming their wisdom, uncovering their deeper meanings, and restoring the sacred complexity that history tried to simplify.

Simondon's theory allows for ongoing transformation, rather than static definitions of identity. Today, the resurgence of interest in demonized deities within occult and esoteric traditions reflects a new phase of individuation—one not born from fear or repression, but from reclamation, integration, and conscious engagement.

Modern practitioners often seek to restore these entities as symbols of empowerment, balance, and resistance. Lucifer becomes a figure of illumination and personal sovereignty. Ishtar, embodying both love and war, becomes a guide for integrating polarities within the self. Baal emerges not as a villain, but as a symbol of defiance against authoritarian structures. In this way, their roles are continually reshaped by the cultural and spiritual frameworks in which they are engaged.

Through Simondon's lens, the demonization of deities is not merely a historical injustice—it is part of a dynamic process of individuation driven by systemic crises and cultural shifts. Far from being passive victims of reinterpretation, these entities are active participants in meaning-making, evolving alongside the societies and individuals who engage with them. They are not fixed. Their identities, powers, and symbolic value are continually negotiated through interaction, intention, and transformation.

This framework also offers an explanation for why different practitioners have vastly different experiences with the same demon. If demons evolve in relation to those who invoke, honor, or challenge them, then each relationship becomes a unique co-creation. One practitioner may find Lucifer to be a stern teacher; another, a gentle illuminator; another still, a rebellious firebrand. These are not contradictions—they are facets of individuation expressed through different relational contexts.

We may never be able to prove these shifts in the demon's essence, but reflecting on them opens up profound spiritual insights: What if they evolve with us? What if we, as part of their individuation process, offer them something as meaningful as they offer us?

In the past, the summoning of demons was often confined to secretive, hierarchical orders like the Hermetic Order of the Golden Dawn, the Freemasons, or similar esoteric societies. These organizations were structured, formal, and heavily guarded by oaths of secrecy—partly to protect their knowledge in times of religious persecution, and partly to reinforce a power dynamic that mirrored both societal and theological hierarchies. Within these structures, demons were seen as dangerous, unpredictable forces—entities to be subdued, bound, or banished. The magician held dominion, using precise formulas and divine authority to compel obedience. Spiritual growth was achieved through control— through mastery over the spirits, the ritual, and oneself.

By contrast, contemporary occultism increasingly emphasizes relationship over domination. Many modern practitioners no longer view demons as adversaries or threats, but as autonomous intelligences—beings with whom one might form collaborative bonds. This shift reflects wider societal changes that favor individuality, mutual respect, and the dismantling of hierarchical power structures.

Simondon's philosophy offers a perfect lens through which to understand this shift. The old model of demonology—transactional, rigid, and exclusive—mirrors a closed system of individuation, where roles are predefined and interaction is limited. The new model, rooted in dialogue, mutual transformation, and co-evolution, represents an open system, one where meaning is created through relationship rather than command.

The democratization of occult knowledge—fueled by the internet, online communities, and accessible texts—has further accelerated this transformation. Solitary practitioners are no longer beholden to secretive orders or elite lineages. They are free to explore, adapt, and innovate—to create deeply personal systems of practice grounded in intuition, lived experience, and direct spiritual contact. This evolution is not just practical—it's philosophical. It challenges the very nature of power in magical practice. The practitioner is no longer a master commanding a lesser being; they are a participant in a living, dynamic relationship, shaped as much by humility and curiosity as by will and intention.

By reimagining demons as teachers, mirrors, and guides, we move beyond the fear-based narratives of the past and toward a more nuanced, respectful, and empowered spirituality. This shift doesn't deny the power or danger of these beings—it recognizes that power is not inherently corrupt, and danger is not inherently evil. Like us, demons are complex, evolving, and engaged in their own forms of individuation.

This reframing is not just academic—it's the central mission of this book. To challenge old dogmas. To explore the grey spaces. To honor the forgotten gods not as monsters, but as beings of profound insight, worthy of respect, curiosity, and connection.

14. The Black Flame Within — A Covenant with Azazel

In this chapter, I want to share something deeply personal—my relationship with Lord Azazel. It's not meant to be a blueprint, but rather an example of how deity work can unfold. If this resonates with you, you can take inspiration from this and adapt it to your own spiritual path, especially if you're drawn to a specific demon or already working with one.

The first time I felt Azazel's presence was through divination. I was using an oracle deck, asking vague questions, flipping through the guidebook— still new to the practice and unsure of what I was even doing. But then, something strange happened. I noticed that someone was answering the questions in my head. Not just intuition or vague impressions—answers. Clear and precise.

Eventually, I asked, "Who are you? What is your name?"

And in response, over and over, I heard the name Azazel in my mind— repeating like a heartbeat.

To give you the full picture, I need to explain why I had turned to divination in the first place. I was going through an incredibly difficult period in my life. I felt depleted, lost, and like I was carrying too much on my own. I had reached that point many of us reach at some stage—where the weight of things becomes too much, and something inside you breaks open. I needed help. Desperately. Even though I was raised in a nonreligious home, I'd always had this quiet hope that something was out there. Something bigger than me. Maybe I didn't have the words for it at the time, but I had the longing. So one night, I called out—not to a god I had been taught to believe in, but to the universe itself. To anything that might be listening. And someone answered.

That someone was Azazel.

In the months that followed, we spoke—often. I began to realize that my psychic abilities had always been there, lingering just beneath the surface, even though I'd done my best to ignore or explain them away. Of course, I doubted myself constantly. I questioned everything. But Azazel was patient. He found ways to show me he was truly there—subtle at first, and then undeniable.

Small things began shifting. Appointments that triggered my anxiety would suddenly be cancelled or moved. Opportunities I hadn't seen appeared. Answers fell into place. One by one, the obstacles in my life began to rearrange themselves—not in some grand, miraculous sweep, but in little moments of synchronicity that built up into something I could no longer dismiss.

And then came the teachings. He guided me through meditations. He helped me understand tarot. He showed me how to work with herbs, and how to weave spellcraft into my art. But above all, he helped me begin to see myself—to truly understand my own worth.

Most demons I've worked with have shown up with the same intention: to help me grow. Spiritually, mentally, emotionally. Their methods may be challenging, even confrontational, but they are always purposeful. This kind of spiritual mentorship is often called shadow work.

Understanding Shadow Work

Shadow work is both a psychological and spiritual practice. At its heart, it's about meeting the parts of yourself that you've hidden, rejected, or buried deep. Carl Jung, the Swiss psychologist who coined the term shadow, described it as the unconscious side of the personality—the aspects we often suppress because they're seen as undesirable or "too much." But the goal of shadow work isn't to fix or destroy those parts. It's to integrate them. To understand that they are part of you. To hold them with compassion and transform them into sources of wisdom and strength.

Working with Azazel has taken me deep into those inner spaces—the uncomfortable ones. He has helped me face my fears, my shame, my anger, and my pain. Not to shame me for having them, but to show me how they hold power when acknowledged and transmuted.

The shadow is the part of you that holds what you've rejected, suppressed, or denied—emotions like anger, jealousy, insecurity, or fear, as well as forgotten desires and untapped strengths. It's everything that has been pushed into the unconscious because it was labeled "too much," "not enough," or "unacceptable."

Shadow work is the practice of bringing those hidden aspects into the light of your awareness—not to judge or fix them, but to integrate them. When you reclaim these parts of yourself, you begin to live with greater authenticity and presence. You become less reactive, less self-critical, and more compassionate—toward yourself and others.

This process often brings buried wounds to the surface: unresolved trauma, unmet needs, inherited beliefs that no longer serve you. It can be painful—but it's also incredibly liberating.

In a spiritual context, shadow work is deeply connected to practices such as witchcraft, meditation, ancestor work, and especially demonolatry. These practices often serve as mirrors, revealing what we've kept hidden. I feel it is important to add, that working with demons can bring shadow aspects to the surface quickly and forcefully. And it can be quite uncomfortable. But this is the essence of shadow work, growth through radical honesty and self-acceptance.

How to Begin Shadow Work

Here are a few practical ways to begin your journey:

Self-Reflection Tools

Use journaling, meditation, or divination (such as tarot or oracle cards) to explore the parts of yourself that feel hidden, rejected, or unknown. Ask honest questions. Be willing to sit with the answers, even when they're uncomfortable.

Observe Your Triggers

Pay attention to the moments you feel intense emotional reactions—especially those that seem out of proportion to the situation. Triggers are often doorways to your shadow.

The demon you work with may even place you in situations that surface these triggers intentionally. For example, you might find yourself suddenly overwhelmed in a crowded space, stirring up memories of a past experience that still needs to be acknowledged and healed.

Seek Guidance When Needed

Shadow work is deep, powerful, and sometimes painful. It is not a replacement for therapy. If you're struggling with mental health issues, always reach out to a qualified professional. Be cautious of self-proclaimed gurus or spiritual mentors who place their authority above your autonomy. True guidance empowers, not controls.

Shadow Work Is a Lifelong Process.

This isn't a one-time ritual. It's a slow unfolding. A spiral path. Shadow work requires compassion, patience, and the willingness to sit in discomfort while healing takes root. There will be layers—some more difficult than others—but with each cycle, you reclaim more of your truth and power.

For me, a significant theme has been my art. I transitioned from creating for others—for recognition, fame, or money—making art to be noticed, rather than for the pure joy of creation. I found myself drawing for likes instead of for personal fulfillment. It took me a long time to understand where that pressure came from, but eventually I traced it back to something small that had lived quietly in my shadow for years.

When I was a child, I loved to draw. Art was the one place where I felt free, expressive, and alive. But that changed the day a teacher told me, bluntly, that I would never be a successful artist. "Maybe you could become an art teacher," she said, "but don't expect to make a living from your drawings." I carried that moment with me, even when I wasn't aware of it. Her words became a voice in my head, quietly shaping my self-worth. I began to believe that my art only had value if others approved of it. That I could only be worthy if I proved her wrong—if I was good enough to be "liked."

Azazel helped me face that wound. He didn't soothe me with kindness; he challenged me to confront it. To ask: Why do you create? Who are you trying to prove yourself to? And when I sat with those questions, when I allowed myself to feel the old grief and disappointment, I was able to reclaim my voice. Not for anyone else. For me.

Self-empowerment is the process of reclaiming your autonomy—recognizing your worth, trusting your intuition, and choosing to live in alignment with your truth. It means stepping away from the need for external validation and instead anchoring yourself in your own inner authority. This path often begins when we confront the ways we've been silenced, marginalized, or blamed for things that were never truly ours to carry.

Azazel mirrors the experience of many: misunderstood, cast out, and reduced to a symbol of blame. And yet, he remaines powerful—resilient, wise, and unyielding.

What the Scapegoat Teaches Us:

 Rejection as Initiation: Being rejected by others—by family, by community, by society—can feel devastating. But it can also be the beginning of your own initiation. The scapegoat is cast out, yes, but in that exile, they often find truth. When you're no longer trying to belong, you begin to belong to yourself.

Embracing the Shadow: The scapegoat archetype is tied to the shadow—to everything that others fear, suppress, or fail to understand. But in embracing what others reject, you gain access to your deepest power. Your rage, your grief, your sensitivity, your strangeness—these are not flaws. They are sacred parts of your being, waiting to be integrated.

Transmuting Pain into Power: True transformation often begins in pain. The scapegoat's journey is one of alchemy: taking the wounds inflicted by misunderstanding or exclusion and turning them into wisdom, self-awareness, and radical self-love. This is the path of empowerment—not in spite of pain, but through it.

To walk with Azazel is to walk with a being who understands rejection, who has stood at the edge of belonging and chosen sovereignty. He teaches us that exile can be sacred, that pain can birth power, and that those who are scapegoated often carry the deepest truths of all.

Your path to self-empowerment may look different than mine—but we all know what it's like to be unseen or misunderstood. And within that experience lies the opportunity to reclaim yourself more fully than ever before.

How to Work with Azazel for Growth

Having explored shadow work in the previous chapter, we now move from the inner landscape to the outer world. Working with demons isn't just about confronting hidden parts of yourself in ritual or meditation — it's about how you live, day to day.

Azazel, and many demons beside him, calls us to become rebels in our own lives: to dare to walk our own path, even when it diverges from what others expect; to challenge the roles, identities, and toxic influences that have held us back; to break free from the chains we didn't even realize we were carrying.

This kind of growth doesn't always happen in grand, dramatic moments. Sometimes, it's in the small, courageous acts: saying no to what drains you, stepping away from people who belittle your worth, daring to express who you really are without apology. Azazel's energy pushes us not just to reflect, but to act — to reshape our lives with the same boldness we bring to ritual.

Growth under Azazel's guidance means learning to carry your rebellion with intention and integrity. It's not about chaos for its own sake; it's about reclaiming your freedom, your voice, your power.

By embracing Azazel's archetypes, you can unlock a deeper understanding of yourself and harness your shadow as a source of empowerment, not limitation. His guidance helps you walk the path of spiritual evolution with courage and authenticity.

In some occult traditions, Azazel is considered a guardian of sacred or hidden knowledge—knowledge that can lead to spiritual enlightenment but also has the potential to destabilize the seeker's worldview. It's not knowledge for its own sake, but knowledge that transforms the seeker, forcing them to confront their own limitations, flaws, and fears. The knowledge Azazel shares isn't limited to intellectual understanding but often involves practical arts that lead to personal transformation. Whether it is the knowledge of magic, divination, meditation, or occult practices, Azazel offers tools that allow the practitioner to transcend ordinary existence and access deeper realms of consciousness. However, these tools often require the seeker to be brave enough to face uncomfortable truths and dark aspects of their own psyche.

By invoking Azazel in your spiritual practice, you may feel prompted to challenge your own limitations—both in terms of personal beliefs and in the context of your spiritual practices. Forbidden knowledge isn't just about uncovering truths about the world; it's about challenging the systems of thought that limit your growth and potential. Azazel's teachings urge you to push beyond societal norms and discover your own path.

His role as a teacher of forbidden knowledge can be harnessed to delve into magical and esoteric practices. Whether it is through divination (e.g., tarot, astrology), spellcraft, or rituals, Azazel can guide you to access deeper spiritual and mystical experiences that are often hidden from mainstream society. He can help you tap into hidden powers and potentials within yourself, such as psychic abilities, intuition, or artistic expression, that may be stifled by societal conditioning or personal doubts.

He embodies the archetype of the rebel who defies authority to bring new understanding. In your spiritual practice, you might find that his energy empowers you to question conventional wisdom and explore alternative spiritual paths. This rebellion is not about rejecting wisdom altogether but about seeking truth beyond the limitations imposed by others. Azazel teaches that knowledge is not always given freely and may require courage and self-exploration to attain.

The transformative power of forbidden knowledge is one of Azazel's greatest gifts. His knowledge is not just about intellectual understanding; it's about changing the practitioner from the inside out. This might involve embracing uncomfortable truths, reexamining your life, or making radical changes in your spiritual or personal journey. Like the myth of the fall, embracing Azazel's teachings can lead to a deep spiritual awakening, one that may challenge your perceptions but ultimately lead to greater freedom and enlightenment.

Azazel and the Black Flame

The Black Flame is often described as the spark of divine consciousness, individuality, and self-awareness that exists within each person. Unlike the divine light associated with submission, obedience, or merging with a higher will, the Black Flame represents personal power, self-deification, inner rebellion, and the pursuit of forbidden or hidden knowledge.

It's not about destruction for its own sake — it's about the fire of transformation, the relentless push to break through limitations and reshape oneself according to one's own will. It stands for awakening the part of you that dares to stand apart, question, challenge, and create.

In this sense, the Black Flame and Azazel are intertwined: both represent the journey of awakening the *self* as the ultimate authority, rather than bending to outside forces.

Black Flame Meditation

This is a meditation that Azazel has tought me, a tool I want to share with you. Find a quiet space where you won't be disturbed. Sit or lie down comfortably, and take a few slow, steady breaths to relax your body. Let the tension melt from your shoulders, your neck, your face. Close your eyes, and let your awareness drift inward.

When you are calm and centered, begin to imagine a small flame flickering in the center of your chest. See its strange, shifting colors — black, tinged with deep blue, edged with ghostly white. This is the Black Flame: the spark of transformation, the fire of the self that dares to change.

With each deep inhale, feed this flame. Breathe life into it. With every breath, feel it grow — slowly spreading through your chest, your shoulders, your arms, your belly, your legs, your head. Let it fill you, warmly and steadily.

At some point, you may sense a spot in your body where the flame hesitates — a place of tension, resistance, or stillness. Gently shift your awareness to that place. In your mind's eye, you see a small wooden chest resting there, beautiful but hidden away, waiting.

Approach the chest. You may already sense what's inside: a memory, a wound, a trigger, a pain you've buried. When you are ready, open it. If it feels too heavy or painful, give yourself permission to view it from a distance, like watching a scene from far away. Acknowledge it. Honor it. You have found a piece of your shadow.

Now, invite the Black Flame to rise. Watch as it burns the chest and its contents — not with cruelty, but with cleansing, transformative fire. The wood crumbles, the ashes scatter, and from these ashes, something new stirs: a dark phoenix, rising, powerful and unafraid. This is you — reborn from the part of yourself you have faced, no longer ignored but accepted.

Sit with this feeling for as long as you need. You may choose to stop here, or continue exploring, seeking out other hidden chests, other locked-away pieces of yourself.

When you are ready to finish, slowly bring your awareness back to your breath, to your body, to the room around you. Open your eyes gently. Take a moment to ground yourself — drink water, touch something solid, or write in your journal about what you experienced.

Working with the Black Flame — especially in deep meditations like this — can stir powerful emotions, memories, and energetic shifts. It's important to care for yourself afterward to ensure you stay balanced and centered. Here are some steps you can follow:

Ground yourself physically. Bring your awareness back to your body. Wiggle your fingers and toes. Press your feet firmly into the floor or your hands onto the surface beneath you. You can also stand up and stretch, stomp your feet, or touch a cool object to anchor yourself in the present moment.

Drink water or eat something nourishing. Replenishing your body with water or a light snack helps settle your energy and gently reminds your system that you are safe and supported.

Journal your experience. Take a few minutes to write down what you saw, felt, or released. Don't worry about making it neat or complete — just let your thoughts flow onto the page. This helps process and anchor the insights you gained during the meditation.

Rest if needed. Shadow work and transformation can be emotionally tiring. If you feel drained or tender, allow yourself space to rest. Take a nap, lie quietly, or engage in a calming activity like taking a bath or listening to soothing music.

Clear your space. If you used a dedicated space for your meditation, consider gently cleansing it afterward — you might light incense, open a window, or simply thank the space for holding you.

Be gentle with yourself. Remember: you are doing courageous work. It's okay if you feel raw, emotional, or even a little unsettled after facing shadow aspects. Treat yourself with kindness, and allow time for integration.

The Mirror of the Pages

Deity work is not just about the moments you spend in ritual, meditation, or reflection — it's about integrating what you uncover into your everyday life. And one of the most powerful tools for doing this is journaling.

Journaling acts as a mirror. It allows you to catch glimpses of parts of yourself that might otherwise slip away unnoticed: fleeting emotions, half-formed thoughts, patterns of behavior, or persistent fears. When you put these onto paper, they become visible, tangible — something you can examine, revisit, and understand.

Writing is not just about recording; it's about *processing*. When you journal, you give yourself a safe space to be honest — brutally honest, if needed — without judgment or outside interference. You create a container where you can meet the shadow self face-to-face, explore uncomfortable truths, and let your thoughts and feelings unravel freely.

More importantly, journaling gives you a record of your journey. Shadow work can feel cyclical or slow at times, but by looking back at your entries, you'll start to see how far you've come: Patterns that once controlled you begin to shift. Old wounds start to soften. New insights emerge where confusion once reigned.

Without a journal, it's easy to forget these subtle changes — but with it, you build a map of your personal transformation.

Journaling is not just about pain or shadows — it's also about recognizing strength. Over time, you will begin to notice moments when you stood up for yourself, when you broke old patterns, when you claimed your power. Writing these down reinforces them, turning them into stepping stones rather than fleeting moments. Remember: growth is rarely a straight line.

Your journal helps you see that the path winds and loops, but it is still moving forward.

By committing to journaling, you give yourself a precious gift: the ability to witness your own becoming. You become both traveler and chronicler, shaping your journey with each word you write. Through the mirror of the page, you meet yourself — shadow, light, and everything in between — and you discover that you were never lost, only unfolding.

When working with a demon, like Azazel, journaling becomes more than just personal reflection — it becomes a living record of your shared journey. Each encounter, each subtle sign, each emotional shift deserves to be written down, not only for memory but for meaning.

A lot of demons and deities often works through subtle nudges: A repeated symbol you notice in dreams or daily life. A sudden realization that cracks open an old belief. A challenge or test appearing just as you were about to retreat. Without a journal, these moments can easily pass unnoticed or be dismissed as coincidence. But when you write them down — when you track the synchronicities — you begin to see the threads weaving through your work. You see patterns emerging. You see where you were and where you're heading.

When you journal your work with Azazel, you claim your role as an active participant in the process of your own becoming. You step into the role of both student and scribe, honoring the sacred partnership between guide and seeker. On the page, you bear witness to your own growth — and you ensure that the journey is never forgotten.

Dictionare Infernal illustration of Azazel

The Teacher and Guide

Azazel is often viewed as a bringer of knowledge, particularly in forbidden or esoteric subjects. His teachings illuminate hidden truths—not only about the universe, but about ourselves.

Working with Azazel in this aspect encourages self-reflection and learning. He pushes you to explore areas you may fear or avoid, urging you to expand your understanding of both your inner and outer worlds.

This can manifest as developing new skills, such as divination or spellcraft, or diving into aspects of your psyche that hold the keys to personal empowerment.

For me, this journey began with tarot—but not through a traditional deck. I was drawn to create my own, and through that process, I uncovered a deeper layer of spiritual connection. Each card became a portal—a lesson not just in symbolism or divination, but in trust. I found myself knowing what to draw, how a certain demon appeared, what colors or symbols to use—without ever having seen them with my physical eyes. It was my first true experience of claircognizance: that quiet, persistent knowing that doesn't need to be proven to feel real. At first, I doubted it. But the more I allowed myself to follow that inner voice, the stronger it became.

Azazel never instructed me to do this. There were no commands or overt messages. Instead, he nudged—gently, persistently—guiding me toward an experience I would only later understand in full. Looking back, I see now how much he taught me without words. It was a kind of subconscious apprenticeship—learning not by being told, but by doing, creating, reflecting. Through that art, I learned to listen to myself.

I discovered that drawing is a form of meditation for me, a bridge between the seen and unseen, the material and the spiritual.

As the project evolved, I was inspired—again, through that inner nudge— to depict demons as representations of the Major and Minor Arcana. This idea, which came in the quiet moments shared with Azazel and Lucifer, changed everything. I began researching the demons I drew, learning their attributes and correspondences, but more than that—I felt them. With every sketch, I pushed through old fears of demonology and opened myself to new levels of connection.

That was when the real shift happened. I received so much gratitude, curiosity, and love from the demons I depicted—emotional impressions that reached beyond the veil. I could feel them responding, watching, even celebrating the way I was seeing them: not as threats or caricatures, but as complex beings worthy of respect and recognition.

Through this act of visual alchemy, I came to understand that art isn't just a tool—it's a ritual. A spell. A dialogue. Every brushstroke became an invocation, every completed card a shared moment of presence.

And through all of this, Azazel remained—silent but supportive. Never controlling, only guiding. It was only through reflection that I began to piece together the quiet structure he had laid beneath my steps. He didn't just teach me how to read tarot or contact spirits—he showed me how to become a vessel for that knowledge, through the medium that made my soul feel most alive: art.

Looking back, I now understand that Azazel never gave me direct orders or spelled things out. He didn't tell me, *"Draw a tarot deck,"* or *"This is how you'll learn."* Instead, he guided me with subtle nudges—through feeling, through fascination, through the quiet pull of inspiration. It was never about obedience; it was about becoming. And through that becoming, I learned to trust not only him, but myself.

Through drawing, I discovered that my art is more than expression—it's communion. A form of *visual alchemy*, where the sacred is translated through shape and shadow, line and light. I learned to recognize my *Claircognizance*—those sudden flashes of knowing that emerged as I drew each demon without needing to "see" them. Every pencil stroke became a meditation, a quiet invocation, a bridge between worlds.

This journey taught me that spirit doesn't always speak in words. Sometimes, it speaks in longing. In the things we love. In what calls to us when the world is quiet. What begins as a creative urge or a strange curiosity might, in truth, be a doorway.

If you are holding a pencil, a card, a ritual knife, or simply a question in your heart—follow it. Allow it to unfold. Not everything will make sense right away, and that's okay. The magic is often hidden in the *reflection*, in the way hindsight reveals the lessons we didn't know we were living.

You don't need to be perfect to begin. You don't need to know exactly who or what you're reaching for. The sacred will meet you where you are—through your curiosity, your courage, and your willingness to *try*. And in time, you'll see how the demons, the guides, the spirits—how they were always with you. Not to give you the answers, but to walk beside you as you discover them yourself.

My Personal Practice

My spiritual path is a deeply personal blend of old Swedish witchcraft, animism, and demonolatry. Rooted in the rhythms of the land and the whispering spirits of nature, my practice is shaped by ancestral traditions but redirected toward my own chosen spirits—demons and gods.

Though I honor and respect the ancient Norse pantheon, my heart was drawn elsewhere. I have built lasting spiritual relationships with entities that resonates deeply with my path. Some might change over time, but most of them will stay throughout my entire lifetime. These are the spirits who have spoken to me, guided me, and become part of my inner cosmology. I have chosen to focus on the elemental connection of the four demons I work with most intimately—Belial (Earth), Leviathan (Water), Loki (Fire), and Azazel (Air)—as the core structure of my practice. This elemental framework offers not only a spiritual anchor but also a dynamic, living system through which I experience and interact with the world. It has taught me that structure doesn't have to mean restriction. It can mean foundation. It can be the sacred architecture that supports freedom, growth, and wild devotion. It's through this elemental lens that I've come to understand both the demons I serve and myself more fully— and it's what continues to shape the living, evolving practice I walk each day.

There is a multitude of associations, teachings, and energies attributed to each demon—archetypal, astrological, historical, and cultural. They can be overwhelming at first. But one of the most grounding pieces of advice I can offer is to begin by focusing on a single aspect that resonates with you. Start with what feels intuitive. For me, working with Belial through the lens of Earth gave me a tangible, embodied way to connect—through gardening, recycling, grounding rituals, and offerings placed directly into the soil. From there, the relationship grew organically.

By narrowing your focus in the beginning—whether it's Azazel's role as a teacher, Leviathan's emotional depth, or Loki's spark of sacred mischief—you allow the relationship to unfold naturally. These spirits are not one-dimensional. They are vast and layered, and they will show you more over time. But like any bond, the foundation is built in small, sincere steps.

Belial – Earth: The grounding force in my life, Belial represents stability, sovereignty, and connection to the physical realm. His energy teaches me how to stand my ground, to be self-reliant, and to honor the material world without being bound by it.

Leviathan – Water: Emotional depth, intuition, and shadowy mysteries flow through Leviathan's presence. He teaches me to dive beneath the surface, to confront what is hidden, and to embrace the power of emotion and transformation.

Loki – Fire: Loki has revealed himself to me as a fire-aligned spirit of change, chaos, passion and raw creative force. In my practice, he is not just a trickster but a bringer of necessary disruption—tearing down what no longer serves so something new can be born.

Azazel – Air: My closest ally and teacher, Azazel embodies intellect, breath, and the black flame of transformation. His domain is that of thought, gnosis, and liberation. As a Priestess of Azazel, I see my role not as one of subservience, but as one of devotion, transmission, and service to his current.

I also maintain a devotional altar for **Lucifer**, not tied to a specific element in my practice, but honored as the Light-Bringer, the bearer of knowledge, sovereignty, and inner illumination. Lucifer is not a patron in the same way as my main team of four, but I offer him my respect and gratitude regularly.

Other demons appear in my practice for specific workings, such as guidance, protection, healing, or creativity. These connections are valuable, but they are more akin to spiritual collaborations than the deep, ongoing relationships I maintain with my core four.

My view on deity work and spiritual practice is grounded in the belief that spirituality should flow naturally into your daily life—not demand that you reshape yourself to fit into rigid systems or inherited frameworks. The Left-Hand Path, and working with demons in particular, is inherently rebellious. It's about forging your own way, refusing to be confined by boxes, labels, or dogmas. I don't follow a system out of obligation—I adapt my practice to reflect who I am, how I live, and the land I'm rooted in. For example, I celebrate spring and autumn not through a pre-defined sabbat, but by planting flowers in the name of Belial or preparing my garden for the coming winter. This simple act connects me to the earth, honors his energy in the soil, and allows me to take part in the raw, sacred cycle of decay and renewal—on my own terms.

This personalized approach is one reason I prefer working with demons. They don't demand conformity; they invite authenticity. They challenge you to create your own rules, to question dogma, and to honor the self as a co-creator of spiritual meaning.

What Is a Patron Demon?

A patron demon is a spiritual ally who walks beside you over the long term—offering guidance, protection, challenge, and mentorship. Much like a patron deity in polytheistic traditions, a patron demon has a more personal investment in your spiritual development. You may build a relationship with this entity through daily offerings, devotional acts, and regular communication. A patron demon is not chosen lightly; often, the connection is mutual. They may appear to you during times of transformation or offer their presence repeatedly until a bond is formed. These relationships evolve, sometimes beginning subtly and deepening over years of shared work and understanding. In many cases, this bond becomes a formal commitment—a spiritual contract or covenant that you consciously choose to uphold over a significant period of time, or even throughout your entire life. Such a covenant is not about servitude but about shared purpose, trust, and spiritual alignment.

What It Means to Be a Priestess of Azazel

Being a priestess of Azazel is not a title I claim lightly. It represents a deep, ongoing relationship that has shaped who I am. Azazel is my teacher, my initiator, and my guide in both magical and personal realms. He came into my life during a time of spiritual upheaval, offering wisdom when I needed it most. Since then, our bond has deepened through ritual, art, divination, and shared silence.

To serve Azazel as a priestess means to embody his teachings and carry his flame into the world—not through dogma, but through example. It means offering support to others who are walking the path of shadow work, rebellion, and spiritual reclamation. It means honoring truth, discipline, and transformation in my own life so that I can hold space for others to do the same.

Azazel has never asked me to worship him. Instead, he has asked me to stand with him—to challenge myself, to confront fear, and to reclaim my power. That, to me, is the essence of priesthood: not obedience, but co-creation.

I have done grand things in Azazel's name—creating an entire tarot deck, an oracle deck, and now this book. These projects are offerings in themselves, born from long hours of study, reflection, and communion with his energy. They are acts of devotion on a large scale, sharing his presence and wisdom with others in creative and enduring forms.

But there is beauty in the small things, too. Sometimes, it's the subtle pressure of his hand on my shoulder just before I step in front of a crowd to hold a lecture, reminding me that I'm not alone. Or the way his

presence wraps around me like a quiet cloak when I feel overwhelmed—
an unseen whisper to take a breath, to ground myself, and to trust.

These moments are just as sacred as rituals or written words. They are
reminders that connection doesn't always have to be loud or ceremonial.
Sometimes, it's as soft as a thought, as fleeting as a shiver down the
spine, as comforting as knowing someone is watching over you—not to
control, but to support.

In this way, my priestesshood is not marked by grand titles or constant
ritual, but by a living relationship. One that ebbs and flows, that makes
space for humanity, for imperfection, and for real life. Azazel does not
demand perfection—he demands truth. And in answering that, I honor
him in every choice I make to grow, to learn, and to walk my path without
shame.

My practice is living, evolving, and rooted in respect for the land, the
spirits, and the shadows. It is shaped by my ancestors and the forgotten
gods who now wear the names of demons. It is shaped by devotion,
discipline, and daily acts of magic—no matter how small.

Some might call me a Left-Hand Path witch. Others might say I'm a
demonolater, a spirit worker, or a practitioner of folk magic. I've used all
of these terms and sometimes none at all. Labels can be helpful for
understanding—but they can also become cages if we cling to them too
tightly.

Walking the Left-Hand Path means carving your own road, not following
one set before you. It's about rebelling against imposed systems, not for
the sake of rebellion itself, but to find authenticity, freedom, and truth.
My path doesn't fit neatly into any predefined category, and that's the
way I like it. I believe we don't need permission to name our path—we
only need the courage to walk it. This is the heart of my demonolatry.

King Belial by Emmy Sollien©2023

VISUAL ALCHEMY – ART AS SPELLWORK AND SPIRITUAL CONNECTION

Visual alchemy is the process of using imagery—drawn, painted, sculpted, or digitally created—as a form of magical transformation. For me, art is not only an act of creation; it is a ritual, a form of divination, a conversation with the spirits, and a mirror reflecting the unseen.

In my practice, visual alchemy is deeply intertwined with my spiritual path. It is one of the primary ways I connect with demons and express my devotion. Rather than only lighting candles or reciting prayers, I sit down with pencil or tablet and open myself to the presence of a spirit. I allow their energy to move through me, guiding the lines, textures, and colors. It is not always about capturing a literal appearance—it's about embodying their essence through art.

Many of the demons I've connected with first came to me not through ritual, but through the quiet act of drawing. I would receive impressions— shapes, faces, feelings—that would not leave me until I committed them to paper. This is a form of claircognizance, or "clear knowing."

I do not always "see" the demon, but I know what they look like, what colors they carry, what symbols surround them. Through the act of drawing, I enter a meditative state that allows these images to take form, often revealing aspects of the demon I had not previously understood.

This is visual alchemy: turning the unseen into seen, the abstract into form, the spiritual into the tangible.

One of the most profound examples of this process was the creation of my demon-themed tarot and oracle decks. The idea was given to me by Azazel and Lucifer—not in a commanding way, but as a suggestion, a seed planted in my mind. As I began to explore this idea, the images flowed naturally. I felt drawn to represent each demon as an archetype from the tarot, associating their energy with the major and minor arcana. The work not only taught me more about the demons themselves, but it deepened my understanding of tarot and the symbolic language of the occult.

Through this process, I received messages from the demons I illustrated—gratitude, curiosity, and love. This changed my relationship with them. It opened doors to spirits I might never have reached through words alone.

Visual alchemy is not limited to grand projects. I also use it in my daily practice—sketching sigils, creating amuletts from clay, or simply creating art that channels a specific emotion or energy I want to transmute. I see it as both a devotional offering and a way to clarify my own inner world. It is a form of spellwork, and also a form of self-reflection.

Visual alchemy is a language, and like any language, the more you speak it, the more fluent you become. You do not have to be a "good" artist to engage with it. The value lies not in perfection, but in presence—the act of showing up, engaging with your spirits, and giving form to your inner visions.

In this way, art becomes more than expression—it becomes communion. A sacred act. A spell. A bridge between the mundane and the divine.

FINAL WORDS - RECLAIMING THE WISDOM OF THE DAMNED

Throughout this book, we've walked through the shifting histories, mythologies, and lived experiences surrounding beings like Azazel—once divine or revered, now cloaked in shadow by fear and dogma. This has not just been an exploration of forgotten stories. It's been a reclamation. A remembering. These beings were not always feared. They were gods, teachers, protectors—figures who once stood beside humanity, offering wisdom and challenge in equal measure. Through time, they were cast out. Silenced. Demonized. And yet—they never truly left. They continued to whisper, to guide, to rise in the hearts of those willing to listen.

For me, writing this book has been deeply personal. It's the result of years spent not just studying or practicing—but living alongside these spirits. Learning from them. Questioning them. Sometimes arguing with them. Always growing because of them.

Working with demons has taught me to see the sacred in the hidden and the holy in the feared. It's shown me that transformation isn't always gentle. Sometimes it burns. Sometimes it strips you bare. But in that rawness, you meet yourself.

This book is not a manual or a doctrine. It's an invitation. An offering of perspective—for those who feel drawn to the edges, to the wild truths outside the bounds of tradition. If you've ever felt like you didn't quite fit, like you were too much or not enough, like the world's rules weren't made for you… you're not alone. The beings in these pages know that feeling intimately. And they can help you turn it into power.

Whether you choose to work with Azazel, Lucifer, Lilith, or another forgotten god entirely, know that the relationship is yours to shape. It doesn't have to look like anyone else's. You don't need robes or candles or Latin invocations (unless you want them). You just need presence. Curiosity. A willingness to go deeper—into yourself, your shadow, your story.

If this book has given you a spark—use it. Follow it. Let it guide you into the dark places, and trust that what you find there is not your ruin, but your rebirth. We are not here to be saved. We are here to remember. To reclaim. To rise. And you are more ready than you think.

With love and in shadow,

Emmy

Further Exploration:

The Demon Profile PDFs

If you feel drawn to deepen your connection with the entities introduced in this book, I've created a series of downloadable PDFs that explore individual demons in greater detail. Each one includes:

A deeper look into the demon's origin, symbols, and historical background
Suggested offerings, altar ideas, and sigils.

Ritual and meditation prompts.

Personal reflections and practical guidance for spiritual work

These are available for download via my website:

🌐 www.emmian.net

Each PDF is designed to help you build a personal and respectful relationship with these entities, honoring both their complexity and your unique spiritual path.

Glossary

Altar – A sacred space used in ritual or spiritual practice, often containing items representing spirits, deities, or elements. In demonolatry, it may be customized to honor a specific demon.

ANE (Ancient Near East) – A historical term referring to the region encompassing ancient civilizations such as Mesopotamia, Sumer, Akkad, Assyria, Babylonia, Canaan, and parts of Egypt, Anatolia, and Persia. The ANE is often referenced in studies of early religion, mythology, and demonology because it was home to some of the world's first written spiritual systems. Many demons, deities, and cosmological ideas found in later Western traditions originated or were influenced by ANE cultures.

Astral Plane – A spiritual dimension beyond the physical, often accessed in dreams, trance, or meditation, believed to be where spirits and entities reside or communicate.

Banishing – A ritual practice to remove or distance spiritual entities or energies from a space. While common in ceremonial magic, it is used more selectively in demonolatry.

Binding (Pact, contract) – A formal agreement between a practitioner and a spirit/demon, often involving terms of exchange. Not to be taken lightly, and always approached with clarity and respect.

Channeling – The act of allowing a spirit or entity to communicate through the practitioner, either through speech, writing, or energy.

Claircognizance – Psychic knowing without prior learning or explanation. A type of "clear knowing" often experienced when working with spiritual beings or receiving intuitive insights.

Covenant – A solemn and intentional agreement or vow between a practitioner and a spiritual entity. In the context of demonolatry or deity work, a covenant often reflects a long-term or lifelong commitment, marked by mutual respect, devotion, and shared purpose. Unlike casual or short-term pacts, a covenant is rooted in trust, spiritual alignment, and deep personal significance. It may include rituals, offerings, and personal dedication, and often evolves over time as the relationship between practitioner and spirit deepens.

Daemon/Daimon – An ancient Greek term for a spiritual intermediary between gods and humans. Unlike later demonized interpretations, daimons were not inherently good or evil.

Demonolatry – The spiritual or religious practice of honoring demons as divine or powerful spiritual beings.

Demonology – The study or classification of demons and demonic entities, often from historical, religious, or occult perspectives. While traditional demonology often viewed demons as evil, modern practitioners may reinterpret it as a framework for spiritual exploration, understanding archetypes, and working with demonic forces.

Divination – A spiritual or magical practice used to gain insight, guidance, or knowledge through symbolic systems or intuitive connection. Common forms include tarot, runes, scrying, pendulums, and oracle cards. In demonolatry, divination may also involve direct communication with demons or spirits, either through tools or psychic impressions. Rather than predicting a fixed future, divination is often used to explore possibilities, uncover hidden truths, or receive messages from spiritual allies.

Elemental Correspondences – Associations between entities (like demons) and natural elements (earth, air, fire, water). Often used in ritual work for alignment or intention setting.

Enochian Magic – A system of ceremonial magic involving angelic beings, developed by John Dee and Edward Kelley. While not focused on demons, it influenced Western occult traditions.

Enns – Short chants or mantras associated with specific demons, used by practitioners to focus intent and open communication with the spirit.

Evocation – The ritual act of summoning a spirit into a space without calling it into oneself, often used in ceremonial magic.

Gnosis – Spiritual or intuitive knowledge gained through direct experience rather than external teachings. Central to many esoteric paths, including demonolatry.

Grimoire – A manual of magical knowledge, rituals, sigils, and spirit descriptions. Many historical grimoires, such as *The Lesser Key of Solomon,* catalog demons and their attributes.

Id – In Freudian psychology, the part of the mind associated with primal urges and desires. It operates on the pleasure principle and is in constant tension with the superego, which embodies internalized societal norms.

Immanence – The belief that divine or spiritual forces are present within the world and the self, as opposed to being wholly transcendent. Important in pantheistic and magical worldviews.

Invocation – A ritual act of inviting a spiritual entity into the practitioner's body or consciousness, often for guidance, empowerment, or communion.

Left-Hand Path Witch – A practitioner who follows a rebellious, self-defined spiritual path rooted in the Left-Hand Path tradition. This approach emphasizes personal empowerment, shadow work, self-deification, and challenging conventional spiritual norms. Often associated with working with demons or darker deities, Left-Hand Path witches value autonomy, transformation, and spiritual sovereignty over conformity.

Libation – A ritual offering of liquid, often wine or water, poured in honor of a deity or spirit.

Pathworking – A meditative or ritual journey, often visualized, used to interact with spirits, explore archetypes, or access spiritual wisdom.

Personal Gnosis (UPG) – "Unverified personal gnosis," a term used in spiritual communities to describe knowledge or experiences received directly from spirits or the divine, outside of established tradition.

Sacred Names – Names or words of power believed to carry deep spiritual or magical significance. In demonolatry, the true names of demons are often used to call upon them with respect.

Shadow Work – A practice of exploring and integrating repressed or hidden aspects of the self, often with the help of spirits or deities.

Sigil Crafting – The creation of magical symbols that condense an intention or spirit into a visual form. Common in chaos magic and demon work.

Sigils – Symbols associated with spirits or intentions, often used in rituals, meditation, or spellwork to focus energy or open a channel to a specific being.

Spirit Work (Deity Work) – A general term for building relationships with spirits, including demons, ancestors, guides, or elementals, through offerings, rituals, or direct communication.

Theurgy – A magical or mystical practice aimed at achieving union with the divine, often through ritual, invocation, or spiritual ascent.

Transmutation – The alchemical or spiritual process of transforming one's inner self. Often used metaphorically in shadow work and demonic mentorship.

Tutelary Spirit – A protective or guiding spirit that works closely with a practitioner. Many demonolaters view certain demons as personal mentors or tutelary spirits.

UPG (Unverified Personal Gnosis) – See Personal Gnosis.

Witchcraft – A diverse set of magical, spiritual, and folk practices often centered around nature, spirits, and the self. In this book, it intersects with demonolatry in various forms.

SOURCES

The Satanic Panic and Modern Demonology

- The Satanic Panic: A Brief History, by Jeffrey S. Victor

- The Satanic Panic: The Enduring Legacy of Hysteria, by R. Kenneth Godwin (1991)

- Devil Worship: Exposing Satan's Underground (1988), Geraldo Rivera

- The Demon-Haunted World: Science as a Candle in the Dark by Carl Sagan

Traditional Religions and Folklore

- Karen McCarthy Brown: Mama Lola: A Vodou Priestess in Brooklyn

- William Bascom: The Yoruba Religion: A Short History

- Barbara E. Barber: Witchcraft, Sorcery, and the Supernatural

- H.R. Ellis Davidson: Gods and Myths of Northern Europe

- Neil Gaiman: Norse Mythology

- S. Connolly: Modern Demonolatry

- Michael W. Ford: The Devil's Bible

Medieval and Religious Studies

- R. I. Moore: The Formation of a Persecuting Society

- Heinrich Kramer: The Malleus Maleficarum

- Ronald Hutton: Triumph of the Moon: A History of Modern Pagan Witchcraft

Ancient Texts and Divine Councils

- 1 Enoch, Chapters 6-16 (The Book of the Watchers)

- The Early History of God by Mark S. Smith

- God in Translation by Mark S. Smith

- Michael S. Heiser: The Unseen Realm

- George W. E. Nickelsburg: 1 Enoch: A New Translation

- John J. Collins: The Apocalyptic Imagination

- William W. Hallo: The Bible and the Ancient Near East

- Terry Watkins: Demonology in the Bible

- McClellan, Daniel O (2022). YHWH's Divine Images: A Cognitive Approach.

Divine Councils and Fallen Beings

- Isaiah 14:12-15 (The Lucifer Passage)

- Zechariah 13:2 (The Unclean Spirit)

- The Bible Odyssey: The Divine Council

- John Walton and Michael S. Heiser: Divine Council in the Hebrew Bible

Demonization and Deification in Ancient Civilizations

- The Infernal Dictionary by Collin de Plancy

- Myths from Mesopotamia by Stephanie Dalley

- The Epic of Gilgamesh and Ancient Near Eastern Religions

- Satan: A Biography by Jeffrey Burton Russell

Zoroastrianism and Dualism

- Zoroastrianism and the Problem of Evil – A study of dualism and its influence on later   Judeo-Christian concepts of evil

- The Birth of Satan: Tracing the Devil's Biblical Roots by T.J. Wray and Gregory Mobley

Occult and Esoteric Texts

- The Book of the Law by Aleister Crowley

- The Book of the Left-Hand Path by Michael W. Ford

- Steganographia by Johannes Trithemius

- Cornelius Agrippa, Three Books of Occult Philosophy

Ancient Mythology and Pantheons

- Ugaritic Texts (e.g., The Baal Cycle)

- Mark S. Smith: The Early History of God

Contemporary Satanism and Demonology

- The Church of Satan – Official website

- The Satanic Temple – Website detailing contemporary Satanism

- American Gods by Neil Gaiman

Further Reading and Reference Works

The Infernal Dictionary by Collin de Plancy

The Encyclopedia of Demons and Demonology by Rosemary Ellen Guiley

Aleister Crowley: The Book of the Law

Ronald Hutton: Triumph of the Moon: A History of Modern Pagan Witchcraft

M.Belanger: Dictionary of Demons. Expanded and Revised: Names of the Damned

Gilbert Simondon: On the Mode of Existence of Technical Objects (1958)

Gilbert Simondon: Individuation in Light of Notions of Form and Information (1989)

Frances Yates, Giordano Bruno and the Hermetic Tradition

Brian Copenhaver, Hermetica: The Greek Corpus Hermeticum and the Latin Asclepius

Paul Oskar Kristeller, Renaissance Thought and the Arts

Marsilio Ficino, Three Books on Life

Lyndy Abraham, A Dictionary of Alchemical Imagery

Paracelsus, The Book of Alchemy

Nicholas Campion, A History of Western Astrology

Johannes Kepler, Tertius Interveniens

Christopher I. Lehrich, The Language of Demons and Angels

Frances Yates, The Occult Philosophy in the Elizabethan Age

Jeffrey Burton Russell, The Devil: Perceptions of Evil from Antiquity to Primitive Christianity

John Dee, Monas Hieroglyphic

Steven Shapin, The Scientific Revolution

Antoine Faivre, Western Esotericism and the Science of Religion

Margaret Jacob, The Newtonians and the English Revolution

Frances Yates, The Occult Philosophy in the Elizabethan Age

D.P. Walker, Spiritual and Demonic Magic from Ficino to Campanella1.0. Titel på kapitlet